AUTHENTICITY?

Erika Balsom
Franco 'Bifo' Berardi
Barbara Cueto & Bas Hendrikx
Jazmina Figueroa
Holly Herndon & Mat Dryhurst
Rob Horning
David Joselit
Oliver Laric
Timotheus Vermeulen
Beny Wagner
McKenzie Wark

Making Public
Valiz

AUTHENTICITY?
Observations and Artistic Strategies in the Post-Digital Age

Barbara Cueto
& Bas Hendrikx
(eds.)

AUTHENTICITY?

CONTENTS

CONTENTS

INTRODUCTION

Barbara Cueto & Bas Hendrikx

Authenticity has become the ultimate asset. Originally, it was linked to the idea of a core of a thing—its essence. Recently, however, as a consequence of globalization and the ubiquity of technology, we are witnessing new ways of creating authenticity and processes of authentication that differ radically from this traditional notion. The longing to be true to oneself has become a cliché. The Internet is deeply embedded in our day-to-day lives, transforming our routines and allowing us to multiply ourselves in avatars and profiles. It is easy to disregard authenticity as just a hollow shell, but its presence and force are undeniable in these times of digital hegemony. How can one be true to infinite scrolling?

There was a promise that access to information via digital means would be democratized, but instead we have seen digital surveillance and an overabundance of images. Moreover, the digital revolution has given way to the post-digital era, which no longer distinguishes between on- and offline, and which embeds and normalises digital technology in almost every personal relation, labour condition or aesthetic practice. And the concept of authenticity has been a casualty of this change: initially clearly defined and with a well-delineated referential scope, it has seen that its sharpness dissolve in the post-digital era.

Prefixing 'digital' with 'post-' moves us, in referential terms, beyond the era before the internet entangled day-to-day experiences with this and that technology, and users hadn't yet lost their naiveté about the implications of using digital technologies in their lives. At the same time, we think 'post-digital' is more apt than 'post-internet', which often describes objects or concepts that find their source online and that are then translated back into a physical form. Instead, post-digital allows us to discuss a wider range of behaviours and processes in which on- and offline are mutually intertwined and which have left an undeniable imprint on society.

Airbnb, the online platform, with its slogan, 'Live Like a Local', has considerably altered the way in which we travel and use our own homes. Many cities, such as Amsterdam[1] and Barcelona,[2] are seeing rising house prices, gentrified neighbourhoods, and the displacement of local communities. The effects being wrought by the digital sphere have also been seen in surprises such as Brexit and Trump's election, which have been enabled in part by phenomena that have been developing for years, such as the decay of print media as a central source of information and the rise of social media and the filter bubble.[3] Even groups such as ISIS make their strategic use of digital media. The effects of digital tools and platforms are constantly present: no longer merely virtual, they can be found in our cities, in government, and in our identities.

The term 'authentic' is used to mean either 'of undisputed origin or authorship' or, less rigidly,

1
Renate van der Zee, 'The "Airbnb Effect": Is It Real, And What Is It Doing to a City Like Amsterdam?', *The Guardian*, 16 October 2016.

2
Stephen Burgen, 'Barcelona Marches to Curb Negative Effects of Tourism Boom', *The Guardian*, 29 January 2017.

3
See Eli Pariser, *The Filter Bubble: What the Internet Is Hiding from You* (London, 2011).

'faithful to an original'. To say that something is authentic is to say that it is what it professes (or is reputed) to be, in terms of its origin or its authorship. But things get more complicated when we discuss authenticity as a characteristic of people.

What is it to be oneself? The question raises metaphysical, epistemological, and moral issues. For Kierkegaard, authenticity relies on religious faith. Nietzsche's atheist interpretation involves seeking truth without the use of virtues. And in existentialism, authenticity depends on the degree to which one is true to one's own character despite external pressures.

The Romantic notion of authenticity was about introspection, about getting to know one's true self. It was an internal process, closely related to the etymological meaning of *autos* (self) and *hentes* (being). This shifted in the post-digital context, where authenticity becomes a process that can be purchased and enacted. We share personal information about our lives, work, and relationships on social-media profiles, trading anonymity for the power of social networking. Authenticity is performed, and requires an audience. The process has been externalised. Authenticity is in the eye of the beholder, so to say. Digital technologies have affected both the nature of identity and its socio-cultural function. While the idea of identity is not synonymous with the idea of self, the post-digital era contributes to a dislocation of identity from corporeal being, thus dismantling the concept of identity and, in turn, the idea of an authentic self. Or, as Chus Martínez puts it: 'By performing the self, one becomes the self.'

It could be said that there is an authenticity industry that constantly attempts to stage the effects of the genuine. Consumers want to acquire the products in which that genuineness inheres. Authenticity is featured as a central concept in brand strategies: businesses rebrand their products as authentic, and buyers respond by crediting themselves with a sense of discernment for buying them. Authentic commodities are similar in some ways to luxury goods, including in the ways they impart privilege. The same level of privilege that it is observed in consumer society is found in the virtual space. The digital sphere is not devoid of schemes of inclusion and exclusion, since the construction of authentic experiences is intrinsically biased because structural oppression, as Jazmina Figueroa points out in her text.

The value of authenticity, as it applies to commodities, increasingly applies to cultural artefacts too. The status of a unique work of art or a heritage landmark has changed. Provenance issues are at play not only for heritage items, but increasingly for digital art and culture as well. The circulation of digital files often increases their value, while erasing dilemmas in terms of origin, which become unimportant when one assesses their worth. Moreover, new tools, including digital tools such as

4
A blockchain is a distributed database containing a continuously growing list of records, each of which is time-stamped and linked to the preceding block. Blockchains are used, for instance, to record transactions in the virtual currency Bitcoin.

blockchain,[4] provide new solutions for authentication.

Historically, there have been two criteria that had to be met in order for something to be regarded as authentic: provenance and content. Authentic objects and personas are original, real and pure: they are what they claim to be, and their origins are known and can be verified: essence and appearance are one. These forms of authenticity are not always appropriate when dealing with the post-digital context, nor are they equally important in all situations. The opposite of each may then be whatever is superficial, false, deceptive, or just new. A revision of both is needed in order for a new framework for authenticity, in its current meaning, to be established. As David Joselit puts it: 'Instead of aura, there is buzz.'

Based on experiences and talks at the Impakt Festival, which took place in October 2016 in Utrecht, the Netherlands, this book is a collection of reflections and observations, from political, social, technological, and artistic perspectives, on contemporary authenticity. In this way, the book turns authenticity into a fruitful point of departure for the analysis and better understanding of changes in the post-digital age.

The book starts with three essays that address the new conceptualization of authenticity as an agent of affect. Timotheus Vermeulen questions the validity of authenticity by contrasting an existentialist notion with one found in one's own subjectivities. Rob Horning explores the allure of authenticity in our consumer society, and delves into how it is perceived and commercialized, in order in turn to reframe the notion of authenticity as a tool for products and personal branding. For his part, Beny Wagner uses memories, metaphors, and pop-cultural references to draw an analogy between the extraction of resources and the extraction of affect and memory from people.

The next three texts in the collection look into authenticity in relation to provenance, tapping into its repercussions in artworks and heritage. David Joselit maps the difficulties of exhibiting cultural-heritage items that have been uprooted from their original find spot. Erika Balsom discusses the comeback authenticity is making in contemporary exhibitions, and interrogates how it is being used and the purposes it is being put to. McKenzie Wark addresses questions around authenticity from by looking at the circulatory value of digital images.

Jazmina Figueroa, Mat Dryhurst and Holly Herndon, and Franco 'Bifo' Berardi each delve in different ways into the political impact of digital technologies for authenticity. Jazmina argues that the constitution of the hegemonic authentic in virtual spaces deletes the position of marginalized groups, thus generating a situation of inherent discrimination. In the interview we conducted with Mat Dryhurst and Holly Herndon, we inquired about the role and influence of technology in their music, life, and work, which bring out the sometimes-latent political undertones of the post-digital condition. Franco 'Bifo' Berardi cites the acceleration of what he calls the 'info flow' as the reason for the saturation of the social mind and the deadening of its critical capacities.

Oliver Laric's 3D scan of a *Double Herm with Epicures and Metrodorus* appears throughout the volume in the form of a flipbook. This open-source file[5] is a scan from the collection of the Institut für Klassische Archäologie in Vienna.

This book explores the position of the new authenticity, and attempts to conceptualize and understand whether it is relevant beyond Walter Benjamin's aura of the original—and, if so, in what ways. In ten texts, essays, interviews, and artists' contributions, it constructs a framework through which to explore contemporary connotations of authenticity. It is an inquiry into its value and relevance—into its status as a fluid, performative process dislocated from concepts such as identity and truth.

5 Available via threedscans.com.

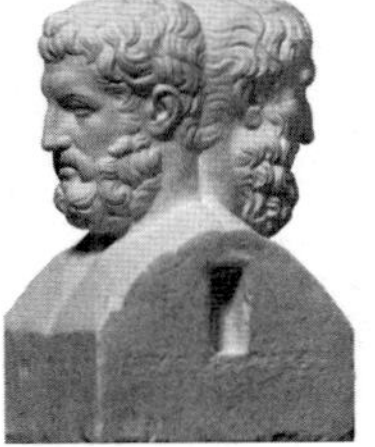

INTRODUCTION

CONTRACTION AND EXPANSION

Timotheus Vermeulen

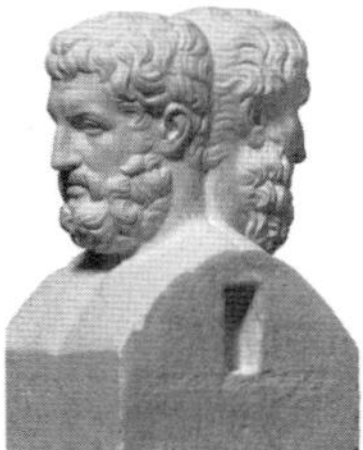

Authenticity seems to me to be a problematic concept, or affect, or phenomenon, or disposition, to write about. Indeed, even figuring out how authenticity should be designated, to what epistemological register it belongs, is troublesome. And that's still to say nothing of its ontological categorization. For authenticity is—even, I would assume, for those who do know, or have in any case decided, what register they are talking about—a slippery something, a gruellingly glib old thing, hard to get a hold of, and exhausting to hold on to once you do.

If we treat authenticity as a concept, are we referring to the theories of Søren Kierkegaard or those of Lionel Trilling, or Theodor Adorno, or punk? What do structuralists make of it? *Can* they make anything of it? And what about materialists? Is the authentic person true to themselves, in spite of external pressures? Or is authenticity precisely to be found in our relationship to something meaningful outside us? Is authenticity necessarily pure—whatever that means—or can it be corrupted? Does it always imply an origin? If we take authenticity to designate an affect, do we think that it's an expression of something deep inside us rather than a relational, surface quality—that it's less an instance of intensity than it is of extensity? As a phenomenon, are we talking transcendence or performativity? Is authenticity a state or a practice? I guess that it's partly because of this confusion that some would suggest we drop the notion altogether, forget about it just like that. Like the police after an accident, they would have us 'move along now, please—nothing to see here'.

To be sure, my point here is not that authenticity is such a troublesome term—that it is, to continue the simile for a moment, such a wreck—that we should just 'move along' and go about our business. On the contrary, I would argue, rather, that this trouble with defining it, with figuring out what we're supposed to do with it, suggests, as Trilling has proposed, that authenticity matters to us, or in any case that it has mattered to us over the past few centuries.

It seems to me, in other words, that we have been so concerned with the crash, with trying to find ways to salvage whatever we can, precisely because we care about the people, and possibly the things, involved in it. In what follows, then, I try to think through what authenticity may mean to us today—what it is we care about, exactly, and why.

As far as I can tell—as I listen in, admittedly, from the margins as opposed to being right there in the thick of things—there are currently two voices that predominate in the debate about authenticity, and that are at once diametrically opposed to each other and serve as each other's corollary—though I'm not sure in the end whether they actually listen to each other that much. The first voice contends, loudly and confidently, that the existentialist notion of authenticity, which has wielded the greatest influence outside the academy and which suggests, crudely put, that authenticity is the *decision* to act as oneself, according to one's own intellectual, spiritual and bodily inclinations as opposed to the pressures of the outside world—has lost its power to convince in the wake of the structuralist and poststructuralist dissections of the dualist subject. Those operations, it tells us, cut open the human skull to discover that there is after all no homunculus inside us to whom we can stay loyal—that there is just a mirror, often concave, or a voice recorder that occasionally skips a beat, diffracting and playing back to us in fragments the discourse of those around us past and present. According to this voice, in other words, authenticity doesn't exist, or in any case not in the way many may have thought.

The other voice I keep hearing is not quite as loud as the first, and is just audible over the hubbub, though it resonates more fully in literary circles. This voice, as one critic, Georgia Christinides, has perceptively put it, asserts that authenticity, understood as our own subjective response to the world, is all we've got left after the disintegration 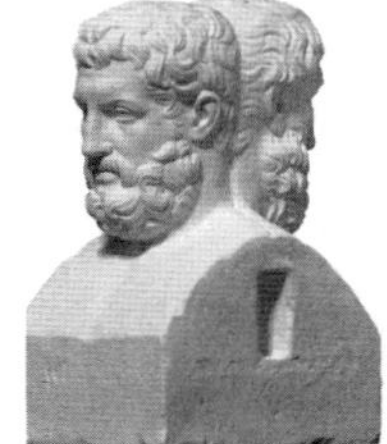

                                CONTRACTION AND EXPANSION

of the genre, or school, of realism, which assumed that one could represent the world objectively, as a totality. After all, not only will my account of reality be different from yours depending on where we are standing or where we each come from—it will also describe a mere fraction of all that we call, rightly or wrongly, 'reality'. For anyone to claim they have unfiltered access to everything would be taken, today, as a joke at best and a clinical disorder at worst (which, to be sure, doesn't keep some from making such claims nonetheless). The authentic act, here, is to share what something feels like to you, as opposed to presuming to explain how it works as a general matter. As Zadie Smith once put it: 'For writers have only one duty, as I see it: the duty to express accurately their way of being in the world.'[1]

You could be forgiven for feeling that these two voices are out of sync, in terms not just of pitch but also of language: one says that authenticity, as agency, no longer exists, that it is not just exhausted as a *concept* but that it should be excised from our conceptual vocabulary. The other says it is only now, in the absence of any objective or universal access to reality, that authenticity has, as *sensibility*, in effect begun to exist. However, as Nicoline Timmer among others has suggested, these two voices do occasionally hit the same notes and plead similar cases, albeit in different languages. The point of the second voice is not that our feelings are our own, either exactly or entirely. For who is to say that our subjective experience— what we feel, what we can feel—is not also always already discursive? Nor is this voice saying that we are in touch with our feelings. After all, why would we assume that we have more access to our own feelings—especially if we treat them as concave diffractions, as fragmented echoes of the outside—than we do to those of others in the world around us? Indeed, authenticity is treated here, not as the expression of an essence, or autonomy or even agency, but as the performance of an emotional resonance, or better yet, of the possibility of emotional resonance—that is to

1
Zadie Smith, 'Fail Better',
The Guardian, 13 January
2007.

say, the cognitivised mode of feeling, the reflective instance, the decision to feel, as opposed to affect.

To suggest that authenticity is performative is difficult to defend in view of the history of the notion—concept, affect, phenomenon, disposition, and so on. Performance is, after all, discursive and relational, whereas authenticity has often been discussed in terms of an essence, an autonomy, or an origin. I would suggest that the notion of authenticity can be used—and is used by some of the aforementioned theorists—in this this context because the performance of emotional resonance transduces discourse from global relationscapes to the most intimate of networks to a point, a position that only your distinct corporeality can inhabit at that very moment. In the performance of emotional resonance, you compel yourself to respond to and reflect on the situation at hand in the context of your particular predicament. Authenticity may not be rooted in a ground, but it is itself an act of grounding. To be sure, by 'point' I do not mean a uniform concretisation. I am thinking, rather, of a diffractive chora, splintering light, or energy, or matter, as it passes through it. The performance of emotional resonance doesn't stop time. It prompts a slippage of time, slows everything down or speeds it up, changes the rhythm in accordance with the particularities of your situation as you perceive it at that moment. It recalibrates time, as Henri Lefebvre might have put it, in terms of your own biorhythm, the rhythm of your biosphere. Or, as Michel Foucault might have said: you are a judoka, redirecting the energy of your opponent somewhere, anywhere, but in any case elsewhere. If those arguing that the model for our present condition is the topology are correct—to be honest, I am not sure they are, but I wouldn't know, at this moment, what other model is more accurate—then the performance of emotional resonance is a simultaneous contraction and expansion that sucks in various lines of flight while swelling up before releasing others. To be

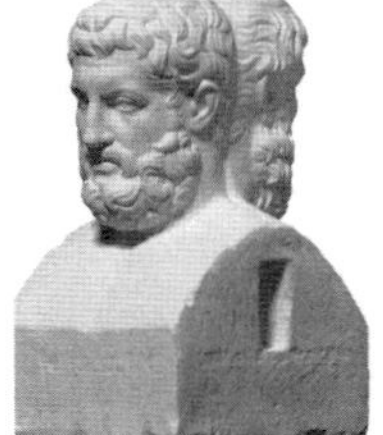

sure, the inauthentic act, in this sense, would be to deny or disavow the possibility of position and operate from a more generalized mood or structure of feeling.

I don't know what the exemplary register of a performance of emotional resonance would be—empathy, passion, trust, hope, or reliance, or even faith. What matters is that it is a register that relates to others, that isn't possible without a relationship to others. For instance, in the act of trusting, you impart part of the responsibility for your corporeal wellbeing, of its past or present or future state, in the hands of the other person or thing or activity. Or, if you empathize with someone, you take on part of that other person's perceived state of mind. In performing emotional resonance, you acknowledge that you are at once the outcome of a social apparatus and its origin, and neither: a relationality, able to resound, to reverberate in multiple ways, each coming from where you imagine or pretend to find yourself at that moment.

Trilling's argument is that, over the last few hundred years, Western culture has gradually shifted its gaze from sincerity as an act to authenticity as a state. It may be tempting to say that, recently, in our post-historical, late-capitalist, Anthropocene, digital times, living with all the fake news and in our echo chambers, we've been sliding back, or around. People speak, after all, of the 'new sincerity': a performance of earnestness. It seems to me, however, that, if we really want to sense the burden of our moment, the weight it carries, and the drag it imposes, we may also want to talk about authenticity, or, as Christinides has put it, this authenticity effect.[2] It is in the act of performing emotional resonance, after all—the act of grounding ourselves where there is no firm footing, only flows, or of imagining anchors whilst floating endlessly, that we experience what it means, for us, to be alive today.

[2] Georgia Christinides, 'Truth Claims in the Contemporary Novel: The Authenticity Effect, Allegory, and Totality', in *Realisms in Contemporary Culture: Theories, Politics, and Medial Configurations*, ed. Dorothee Birke and Stella Butter (Berlin, 2013), pp. 33–48.

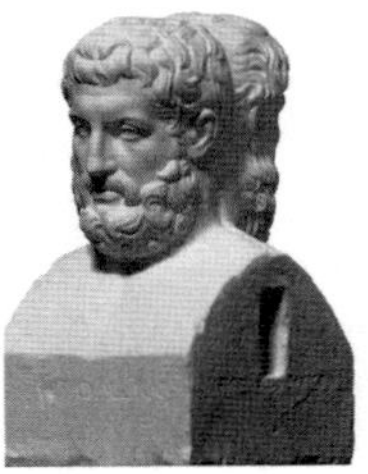

CONTRACTION AND EXPANSION

MASS AUTHENTIC

Rob Horning 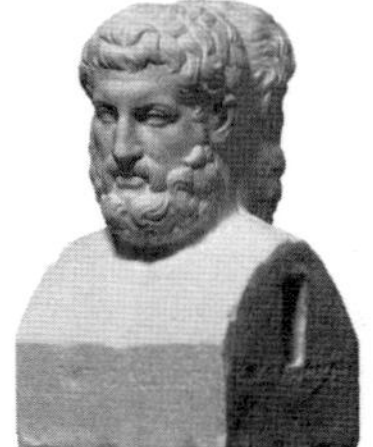

The Authenticity Dream

Why can't we get rid of the idea of authenticity? It seems as if it settles like a fog, blanketing everything with an amorphous sense of inadequacy. It can feel like it refers to everything and nothing.

I want to start with this passage from the introduction to Sarah Banet-Weiser's 2012 book *Authentic™: The Politics of Ambivalence in a Brand Culture*. I think it gets at some of the reasons why the quest for authenticity is so effective as an ideology, even as it a bit of a conceptual contradiction:

> Even if we discard as false a simple opposition between the authentic and the inauthentic, we still must reckon with the power of authenticity—of the self, of experience, of relationships. It is a symbolic construct that, even in a cynical age, continues to have cultural value in how we understand our moral frameworks and ourselves, and more generally how we make decisions about how to live our lives. We want to believe—indeed, I argue we need to believe—that there are spaces in our lives driven by genuine affect and emotions, something outside of mere consumer culture, something above the reductiveness of profit margins, the crassness of capital exchange.

I agree. We do want to believe, despite the many, many ways in which authenticity is misused and contorted in marketing discourse, that there is an authentic realm outside 'mere consumer culture' and its presumably shallow satisfactions, and outside 'capital exchange' and its calculating instrumentalism. We know that there must be a place that facilitates our human flourishing and permits us to lead rich, fulfilling lives. Beyond 'the simple opposition between the authentic and the inauthentic' is the fundamental desire to experience 'genuine affect and emotions'.

But this hasn't gotten us very far. Restating the authenticity ideal as acting on the basis of 'genuine feelings' merely raises the question: What makes feelings genuine?

Is it because they are spontaneous? Is it because they are not motivated by gain? Is it because they are not mediated? Is it because they are witnessed?

It feels as though Banet-Weiser's phrasing simply re-enacts the ideology of authenticity even as she critiques it. Her view seems to be that there is a real, static, correct way of understanding authenticity that can be distilled and separated out from the corrupted uses, just as there are 'genuine' emotions that are unmixed, or 'pure' spaces where desire is uncorrupted by conflicting or competing aims. She seems to suggest that there can be 'authentic' and 'inauthentic' ways to talk about authenticity.

The concept of authenticity, particularly as it is used in marketing discourse but also more generally, is often conflated with a static sort of truth, but invoking it is actually a destabilizing manoeuvre. This conflated version uses an indefinable notion of genuineness to call into question what we might otherwise have taken for granted. It calls into question the inherent genuineness of any affect or emotion in any situation, and undermines any talk of real desires for realness, any authentic way of being authentic that is uncorrupted by the ruses of authenticity. It calls for a sceptical, conspiratorial attitude toward the world, towards other people, and especially toward oneself, construing the 'genuine' as hiding, as forever outside the realm of lived experience. It conveys a sense that we have forgotten how to live properly. The rhetoric of authenticity comes to the fore when what could be true seems especially vulnerable, debatable, difficult, riven, up for auction or appropriation—but authenticity doesn't shore up truth: it exacerbates our doubts about it.

Authenticity, it is claimed, stands for the truth behind the curtain, but it is really just the curtain.

The presumption that only some feelings in some situations are real, and other feelings, though they are actually felt, are somehow false, is authenticity's main ruse.

It would seem that, if we were all striving for a world outside consumerism, this would threaten capitalism as we know it. But marketers actually rely on the idea of 'real spaces' outside consumer culture that we are supposed to yearn for. They don't fear those spaces—they nurture the idea of them. These spaces are the basis of all authenticity-driven advertising: the promise that we must consume our way back to the secure place where our feelings become real and unconflicted again.

Authenticity Simplifies

The idea of authenticity expresses something that never was—uncomplicated, self-evident feelings, identities, experiences—as something that is understood as always already having been lost, in order to promise that we are on the cusp of reclaiming it. Seeking authenticity is always aspirational.

Like 'golden ages' generally, authenticity can be identified retrospectively only: in the past I was 'genuinely myself', but now all I have are elusive memories of that fleeting experience—and perhaps the brands and products that help me articulate that feeling of loss and make it seem recuperable. Authenticity takes the complex cross-currents of my relations, desires, and behaviour at any given moment and simplifies and orients them: the complexities I am experiencing are 'inauthentic' and can be jettisoned in my pursuit of my real self, which I will know just because it is self-evident.

The tenacity of 'authenticity' as an ideological talisman—as a motive force and a *post hoc* explanation for what I've done, as an all-purpose aspiration and excuse—stems from how it posits what it purports to merely describe. It seems to denote 'genuineness', as though it were simply a rhetorical equals sign, a blunt tautology.

It offers a promise of 'truer' alternatives to the messy facts of *what is*. But these alternatives are fictions, not inner truths on the cusp of revelation. They are speculations seeking substantiation at the expense of what actually is.

Authenticity as Escape

In the hands of humanist philosophers such as Charles Taylor or social critics such as Marshall Berman, a commitment to 'authenticity' refers to the effort to foster a society that makes it possible for individuality to emerge For them, 'authenticity' means coming to terms with an inherited set of assumptions about what constitutes a meaningful life, and with limits and horizons we don't choose but grow to work within and preserve. A similar idea from folklore studies suggests that to be authentic is to belong to one's culture as a generic representative.

Those idealized versions of 'authenticity' play into how the concept has been operationalized in marketing discourse, where the emphasis on individuation is married to consumerism but divorced from the complexities of social relations. Currently, the point of seeking authenticity is no longer to build or sustain a society that makes individuality possible but to escape from the supposed constraints society places on the self, mainly through an imagined association of oneself with things.

Rather than use 'authenticity' to acknowledge the tension between individualism and the social norms that permit it to flourish, marketers have seized upon the concept to try to disguise that tension or resolve it through gross simplification. In their hands, authenticity is employed to encourage us to think that we are unique, different, but not so different that we are perceived as alien or threatening. Authenticity allows us to think of ourselves as singular, but with that singularity remaining somehow deeply sympathetic.

From this point of view, feeling compromised by the demands of the social, or consumed by conflicting, irresolvable desires of one's own is a mark of inauthenticity rather than of an accurate appraisal of one's condition. Rather than confront the ways in which we want what other people have or are consigned to compete with others, even as we cooperate with them, or the way in which identity is conditioned inescapably by histories of oppression, injustice, violence, and hierarchy, we can focus instead on a purely personal crisis: a self that really is pure but that we have lost touch with somehow. Doing this simplifies an otherwise irreducible complexity, and gives us an evocative vocabulary with which to talk about how we fit into society while not engendering in us any sense of responsibility for changing it.

Authenticity versus Society

Authenticity in marketing discourse presupposes the unique individual we were all supposed to be according to eighteenth-century thinkers such as Rousseau and Herder, and pits that individual *against* society, which is no longer seen as the source of and grounds for individuality—no more folk culture or tradition, they are strictly in the past—but instead consists of standardized, bureaucratic, massified, synthetic culture. 'Authenticity' becomes commercialized nostalgia for a way of life that never was, and in which we supposed to have experienced no ambivalence.

But, even as it obsessively conjures a nostalgic vision of a world outside it, 'authenticity' is always internal to the culture of consumerism. Though it evokes the lost truth, it is never that truth itself. It is, in fact, truth as lost.

Authenticity emerges in marketing discourse as both a critique of and a consolation prize for consumerism and modernism. It reconfigures an old Romantic ideal whereby one chooses one's own life, and finds the purpose of life by uncovering one's originality, and translates that into consumerist terms, according to which one chooses one's own clothing brands and one's favourite foods. We consume authenticity as though it made the integrity it has promised consumable as well.

Thus authenticity doesn't point to or reconstitute any

experiences that we've lost touch with through the relentless and implacable advances of consumer culture. Rather, it structures in simple terms how we imagine what those experiences might have felt like. It gives an idea of the past that is to be consumed in the present. In the process, it represents what are contemporary consumerist values as if they really came from tradition, as if they were really external to consumerism and could ground it and give it some transcendental meaning: *You really can consume your way to being real! Your brand really can be authentic!*

Authenticity as Real Subsumption

'Authenticity', then, is not something brands are leeching from. It a wholly *ersatz* experience they are making. As Banet-Weiser argues, 'Explaining brand culture as a sophisticated form of corporate appropriation … keeps intact the idea that corporate culture exists outside—indeed, in opposition to—"authentic" culture.' It's not that old forms of authenticity still exist and that capitalism figures out a way to exploit them—a process Marx called 'formal subsumption' with respect to labour processes. Rather, authenticity as we know it issues from consumer culture in a process of 'real subsumption': it is fully integrated with consumerism's workings and integral to its perpetuation. We can't conceive of authenticity independent of the function it serves in consumer society.

If 'authenticity' evokes 'spaces in our lives driven by genuine affect and emotions', as Banet-Weiser puts it, that is because, under consumerism, such spaces have become tangible, concrete commercial properties—new spaces of experiential possibility that are internal to consumerism. Authenticity is ultimately not a measure of the degree to which something eludes commercialization. When something is 'authentic' it is not 'outside of mere consumer culture'; it is, rather, the apotheosis of that culture.

Authentic Goods, Authentic Selves

'Authentic' things, then, are not those goods that evade branding or commercialism. Rather, only brands, only things for sale, can be 'authentic'. When we examine our own 'authenticity', we think of ourselves in the same terms, constituting ourselves as a clearly defined personal brand capable of being convincingly sold.

Because authenticity is tautological (it is what it is), it must be routed through 'authentic goods' that make it tangible for an audience who can then validate the proposed equation. This reduces to a gesture, to something that can be bought and displayed, the experience of a lived relation to others who make it possible for one to recognize one's life as real and meaningful. ('This ethical water bottle instantiates and epitomizes the relations I want people to have with me.')

Authenticity as Scarcity

As marketing consultants James Gilmore and Joseph Pine emphasize in their treatises on authenticity, the concept is fundamentally a means for imposing a perceived scarcity on otherwise satiated consumers. It therefore has nothing to do with a good's physical properties or utility—aspects that refer to demands that can be satisfied. What 'authenticity' appears to make scarce is the sense of self, with 'authentic' goods as the means of reconstituting the plenitude.

Authentic goods position their target consumers as continuous with the products' impossible promise of mass-produced uniqueness, while seducing them with the possibility of easy, individualistic solutions. But that doesn't address the actual sources of anxiety and ambivalence—it merely circulates a sign of authenticity while increasing economic activity. The failure to deliver doesn't undo the overall quest for authenticity, however—it simply intensifies the feelings of inauthenticity that drive such consumer behaviour.

Because the quest for authenticity is fundamentally incoherent—a quasi-mystical attempt to discover something intrinsic to the self—it forestalls any critique on the basis of logic, or empirical results, or cause and effect. Once you entertain the idea of becoming more authentic, you have exposed your basic lack of true authenticity without invalidating it as a life pursuit.

In pursuing authenticity, we become complicit in consumer desire and its mystifications of our social condition. If am concerned about my authenticity, I am not escaping the effects of consumer culture on me as much as I am escaping into them—looking for solace in the simplified terms of brand messaging.

Authenticity as Ambivalence Management

The protocols of authenticity take the complicated ways in which selves are bound up with the inevitable disappointments of social life—its conflicts and rivalries, and the struggles for recognition and distinction—and reduce them to a dichotomy between real and fake. In that way, authenticity forms an intelligible structure that supports what Lauren Berlant calls 'the management of ambivalence'.

Authenticity offers a kind of compensation for a way of life—consumerism—that structurally forbids personal satisfaction. You always have to want more—consumer demand must continually be stoked. Authenticity rationalizes and personalizes that process. Our consumerist dissatisfaction becomes an integral part of personal growth.

We can try to address our ambivalence with performances of self that are ultimately directed at ourselves as the audience, and in which we try to persuade ourselves that we are getting closer to our true self, to something no one else can question. But it is difficult to perform magic tricks on oneself.

Authenticity as Legibility

What authentic goods permit is not the restitution of the self but ongoing self-consumption. They don't heal the subject—they allow one to contemplate oneself as an object, or a medium, a whiteboard on which one can scrawl one's preferred beliefs about oneself. In other words, goods are 'authentic' when they evoke a self-conscious subjectivity permit you to revel momentarily in the fact that you are who you are. We can see ourselves becoming progressively more legible. These goods let us consume as an ephemeral but definite thing the promise that we have a real self in the first place. This is both our reward and our punishment for ever having doubted it.

I may 'need to believe' that my 'real feelings' are anti-commercial or anti-capitalist, but that belief resolves nothing. The tensions we inhabit remain. Meanwhile, the more strongly I insist on having my opposition to the 'crassness of capital exchange' acknowledged, the more I am under the sway of consumerist ideology. The feelings feel real *because* they are commercialized, because they circulate within the channels carved out by capital flows and networks.

Intimate Publics

Part of how consumer society reproduces itself is to commercialize prominent forms of social recognition. The way authenticity is deployed across a range of products, brands, and brand strategies allows commercialized feelings to appear as *more* substantial, *more* shared, *more* real. In consumer culture, safe spaces, as Banet-Weiser argues, are branded spaces: oases of familiarity that convey feelings of security, stability, and belonging—they are harbours of 'utopic normativity' that function as the lost ideals of communal folk culture once supposedly did. They are what Lauren Berlant calls 'intimate publics', in which 'consumer participants are perceived to be marked by a commonly lived history'.

Brands seem authentic when they let us feel as though we belong without blending in. We are able to feel 'normal' because of the visibility of brands we associate ourselves with. This normality has more to do with feeling oneself to be 'authentic' than the narratives of personal distinction that are often associated with authenticity marketing.

'Authenticity' functions by harmonizing the desire to belong with the desire to be unique. Its slippery incoherence is what allows us to find comfort in it.

We aspire to authenticity because it promises recognition without any of the associated limitations or responsibilities. Goods that signify authenticity minister to such fantasies about community and individuality, and posit consumers as generic and unique at the same time.

A few years ago, Carles, of Hipster Runoff fame, depicted what this sort of thing looks like now, with a post about 'the Contemporary Conformist', who pursues studied nonchalance:

> Wood. 'Weathered.' Exposed Brick. Zany Light Fixtures. Hints of Metal. Plants (but not generic flowers). Plaid. Gingham. Denim. 'Chambray.' Shirts with subtle stripes. Contemporary Conformists wear loud neutrals to try to shock you with their naturalism.

Such trappings of authenticity give shape to a kind of intimate public: in Berlant's words, intimate publics 'offer the simplicity of the feeling of rich continuity with a vaguely defined set of like others'. They typify the 'constantly emplotted desire of a complex person to rework the details of her history to become a vague or simpler version of herself'.

Again, authenticity works as an ideology because it simplifies identity and manages our ambivalence about it. Pursuing authenticity doesn't necessarily make us deeper or more complex; it makes us more superficial, more predictable, more easily controlled.

Authenticity as Domination

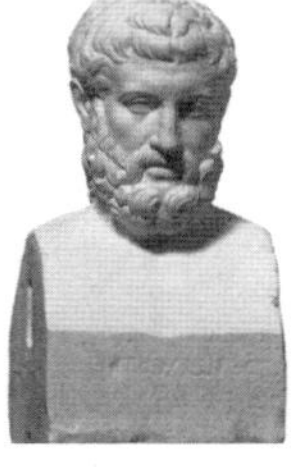

The most effective 'authentic' goods evoke a mainstream ethos from which they nevertheless seem to stand distinctly apart from. This is why they are often products of cultural appropriation.

Just as authenticity posits a split self, it also establishes a distance between a commodity and the ideal it has been positioned to evoke. It inserts itself in the gaps that already exist in the social fabric and justifies them, rationalizes them, allowing the distance between a an othered and a mainstream perspective to become a concrete property, something that can fluctuate in value. The authenticity we consume is often someone else's exclusion, commodified.

The goods that read as authentic are those that allow consumers to flaunt how they can present their consumer choices as decontextualized, as capable of signifying a 'real self' regardless of the circumstances in which they are presented. But they also make a 'real self' contingent on the distance it can sustain between itself and the social milieu that is both a necessary audience and a threatening, subsuming mass.

Given the tension between self-expression and the audience required to make that expression meaningful, authenticity often appears to be measured in terms of freedom from the constraints others place on you. This makes it seem a zero-sum game. The more 'convenient' you make your life, in terms of avoiding interpersonal contact, the more 'authentic' it can feel. But this same strategy isolates people from the social interconnectedness that makes authenticity seem worth the trouble.

The convenient shortcuts to identity are available only to those who are being 'inauthentic', but authenticity is also understood as the ability to reject the conditioning of other people's judgments. Embroiled in this confusion, we feel licensed to assess the authenticity of others across any social distance. We perceive someone else's apparent authenticity, their apparent belonging to a community, as our own inauthenticity. But this doesn't mean that this perception is necessarily generous. Rather, judging someone else as authentic is an assertion of domination, because to be 'authentic' (instead of struggling to become authentic) is to be a product. Feelings of inauthenticity are an authorization to vicariously consume others' experiences as commodities. This has the side effect of de-authenticating that same experience for these others, while confirming and reifying their otherness.

Authenticity is a curse we inflict on other people, and that traps them in their identity while we are free to shop around for ours, claiming tokens of theirs as our own.

But this sort of scrutiny targets us as well. Social media, as I will show in a moment, lets us consume ourselves.

In this process, being authentic and seeking authenticity are framed as mutually exclusive conditions. Being authentic makes you an object that spontaneously and inadvertently displays its essence. Being inauthentic makes you a subject, albeit a devious and strategic one, even though you still seek authenticity. Harmonizing these calls for disavowal—an ability to forget one's inauthenticity in the search for the authentic.

Authenticity turns out to be 'the reward for suspending disbelief', as sociologist Sarah Thornton puts it. It's a form of self-imposed gullibility. That means it is quite far from 'recovering the unique self within'. It also permits us to suspend our disbelief in consumerist magic more generally, and suggests that we can be infinitely malleable.

Authenticity marketing lets us indulge the fantasy that what we buy can truly change our essential nature, even as we persist in believing we are merely expressing that nature.

Berlant sees an intimate public as achieving something similar: it 'produces an orientation toward agency that is focused on ongoing adaptation, adjustment, improvisation, and developing wiles for surviving, thriving, and transcending the world as it presents itself'.

Authenticity as Neoliberal

That sort of flexibility suits a neoliberal structuring of society, in which, to cope with a fully marketized society saturated with competition at every level, we become malleable and continually try to expand our human capital and make our identity productive. The search for authenticity finds expression as self-neo-liberalization.

Insofar as authenticity organizes an intimate public, it prepares us to find fleeting solace in constant self-revision, in the process complementing a sense of underlying stability with ongoing flexibility. The pursuit of a 'real self' rationalizes all the remoulding. Seeking authenticity becomes, not resistance to capitalist exploitation, but a form of surrender to it, with one's entire personality given over to various forms of exploitable labour. The validity of one's 'true self' is confirmed by the fact of being employable, of being available to be put to use.

In managing our ambivalence towards authenticity, we commit ourselves to endlessly managing our personal brand, valorizing authentic goods, performing emotional labour, circulating tokens of 'realness', building up quasi-professional networks, and generating new circuits of value. Self-realization becomes alienated at its core, as personal creativity becomes indistinguishable from an ongoing job interview. This is why Frédéric Lordon suggests that the artist—'the very emblem of free will and the unreserved commitment of the self'—has become the 'avatar' of the ideal employee in neoliberal society.

The fusion of neoliberalism with authenticity has found its full flowering in social media, where enormous quantities of labour are volunteered and harnessed, and self-presentation is foregrounded as entrepreneurial human capital development. Social media, which specialize in collapsing the generic and the particular, friends and strangers, are at once a perfect space for organizing an intimate public around authenticity and for marshalling labour around an ongoing project of self-branding. We manage our ambivalence one social-media post at a time, and allow the decontextualized response the posts receive from no one in particular to serve the managerial role of impelling or redirecting our efforts.

Know Your Production/No, You're Product

It's common to critique social media by pointing out that, while users may believe they are consumers, they are in fact the product, an audience that has been packaged and labelled and is being sold to marketers, who are the real 'users' of ad-supported social media. Or worse, users are both the product *and* the labour that makes the product, all for the benefit of the social-media companies—the owners of the current means of identity production. This means we are not merely deluded but also exploited when we think of ourselves as consuming social media.

The assumption in that critique is that we want, not to be a product, but only to have the agency and the powers of autonomous expression that social media seem to promise. It is thus that users sign up on Facebook with the goal of expressing themselves and following what their friends have to say but are eventually warped into becoming a kind of reified personal brand through exposure to the product's toxic affordances of self-quantification.

Naive users think they are signing up for a personalized public sphere and then, undeterred by the evident oxymoron, find themselves in a hall of mirrors in which all they can see—and all they end up wanting to see—is themselves.

But this analysis doesn't seem to be able to explain the pleasure that users derive from social media, even as those media become reifying and exploitative. What the ideology of authenticity ultimately allows is for users to enjoy becoming the product.

The services that social media supply (having a 'graph' of one's social connections; amassing and archiving personal data; making the promise of an on-demand audience for oneself plausible; permitting a variety of pre-formatted modes of self-expression; offering algorithmically constituted recommendations of what you should read, whom you should know, how you should spend your time, 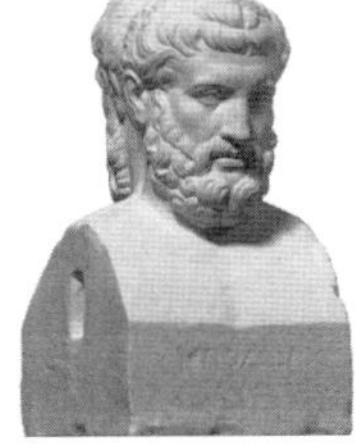

and so on) help constitute the self as something 'authentic' that a user can consume. On social media, we are not on a hopeless quest to integrate our identity but are instead dividing into a self that can watch over itself. We see our authenticity unfold in how social-media interfaces change to accommodate us.

We get to be a commodity and to consume it at the same time. We are like a hot dog putting ketchup on itself.

Authentic Surveillance

This self-commodification does not diminish the user's self-conception but rather makes the self conceivable, legible. Exercising agency no longer threatens one's authenticity. If being calculating, unspontaneous, manipulative, phony, and so on., threaten the integrity of the self, the self as product can be seen as something that simply is, a given thing articulated in a definite form. It enters the realm of the socially conspicuous. It is authentic rather than trying to be authentic.

The self presented to us through the algorithmic processing of our data becomes the most authentic self possible, and from whose construction we have been excluded. It appears as the 'real us' because we can absolve ourselves of having strategized in order to produce representations of it.

This puts digital surveillance in the service of authenticity, as it gathers the data behind our backs and makes sure we don't 'corrupt' it with our conscious intentionality. The data thus collected allows us to know we are leaving an impression regardless of whatever effort we do or don't make.

Extensive surveillance of the self and the 'end of privacy' appear far more tolerable in this light, much as attaching metrics to social interactions in social media makes social stalking and spying seem only natural. This is in keeping with the basic principle of social media: only by being watched can we see who we really are.

Surveillance will let us chart the path to 'being natural' without immediately feeling unnatural about it. Our data gets processed, and what we really want to know, or how we really want to be, is presented to us encapsulated in product form.

Only as a product can we recognize ourselves as 'genuinely' real, given the amount of attention and effort collectively directed at making products seem enchanting and giving them a kind of emotional resonance within a consumer-capitalist culture. We are ideologically trained, every day, to love consumer goods; naturally we would want to become a consumer good ourselves, to appear deserving of love—from ourselves as well as from other people (who, on social media, offer quantifiable tokens of that deserved love in the form of likes and so on).

Products in consumer-capitalist culture quickly lose their lovability, however, as they lose their novelty. They become moribund. They become trash. The self, as a product, loses its enchantment for us and needs to be revitalized to the extent that it becomes familiar, known, understood. We love ourselves only as a novelty, a mystery, not as a staple product. We want to be able to apprehend ourselves as a new, desirable thing that we can consume and enjoy. On social media, we can imagine someone buying into the idea of us, and that helps us buy into ourselves. But inevitably our desire for ourselves needs to be renewed, and we will need to be repackaged.

Authentic Purging

It is untenable to feel authentic only when you're surprising yourself. Social media try to make this contradiction seem coherent. They offer ways in which to continually consume ourselves anew *as* new. Algorithmic recommendations in particular cater to this hope of seeing a stranger in the personal data we've generated, an alien person we can claim as a real self. They can enlarge our ability to desire (thus making us grow) while seeming to

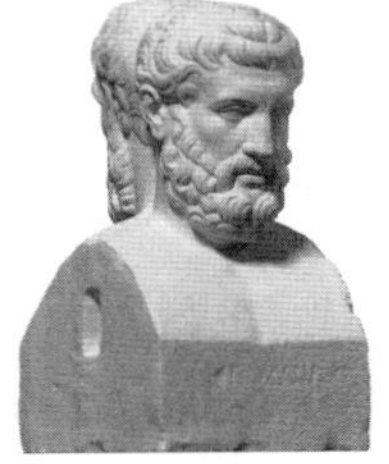

draw on correct information about us that we have passively provided. Everything we have consumed, expressed, and expelled online gets purified and re-presented as new desires, a new 'us'.

By processing our personal data into things such as Facebook's newsfeed, algorithms can present us with a carefully repackaged self. We then get the thrill of unpacking ourselves and seeing what surprise awaits within. That this box we are continually rewrapped in is also a cage can thus be more readily excused. In that cage, we will see only what reinforces the central importance of novelty, but it won't matter as long as we feel new ourselves.

The way our data is processed and represented to us is usually seen as a form of hypertargeting that treats us as a demographic of one. But it is more indicative of the ways in which we are standardized so we can be processed through the same procedures, in order to be socially included. The processing offers a way of belonging. It addresses the same anxieties that authenticity addresses: about how to be a person in general and a particular person, all at the same time.

The self presented back to us can serve as a simplified guide to how to be ourselves, in a version of selfhood that has been pre-approved and pre-certified, but that is also less than fully defined and delimited, and that consists mainly of things such as product recommendations and crude assumptions about what sort of information we are presumed to want to know. It is a set of generic conventions for us as a genre. We can become more authentic in relation to this algorithmic prediction of ourselves, and know exactly what the network expects us to know, while taking a secret pride in the ways in which we exceed those expectations. This self defines a negative space that doesn't have to be part of our human capital, our 'authentic self', or our identity. Our data selves are authenticated, so we don't have to be.

When our social-media profiles can be authentic in our stead, authenticity becomes a matter of quantified attention and of network prominence, rather than of self-consistency.

If we are liked or retweeted, or even if we are given a tailored set of recommendations or push notifications, that signals that we have been consumed appropriately, that our information has been received and is regarded as real and legitimate. That self is a matter, not of expression but of circulation. The content expressed doesn't need to be original or spontaneous or true. Rather, it is just a pretext for measuring the circulation, which becomes the 'authentic' expression of one's situatedness within a network.

Authenticity ceases to be a performed absence of performance, and becomes a matter of *efficient* performance and broad circulation. It thus feeds a loop that reinforces the centrality of networks and fulfils the requirement that we be constantly connected.

Discovering the truth about oneself is not about clarifying the permanent picture of one's sense of self (as if it were an eternal, underlying thing waiting to be unearthed and communicated). Rather, it is about clearing a space and simplifying subjectivity in the present moment, about finding relief from the burden of selfhood, particularly when the self is regarded as 'human capital'.

Social media offers a repository for that capital, and for its authentication, and takes responsibility for how it is put to use. It takes authenticity out of our hands.

What is seen as authentic is something that is no longer our fault. The 'truth' about our selves is final only while it is circulating, and can be forgotten as soon as it ceases to be productive. The most authentic self is the slate wiped clean.

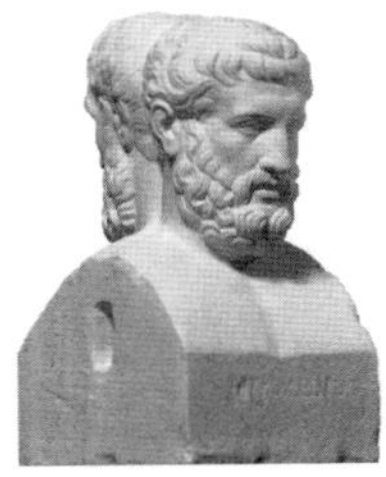

THE MIRACLE-INDUSTRIAL COMPLEX

Beny Wagner

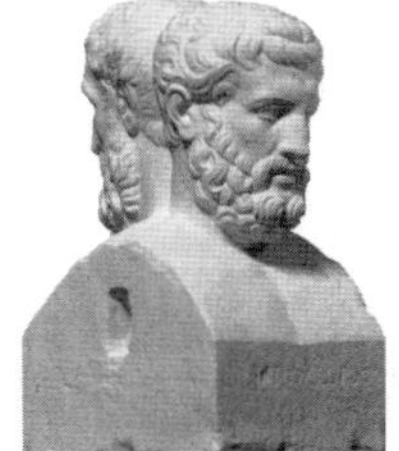

Over the past couple of years, I keep returning to these two sentences by Robert Musil:

> A metaphor contains a truth and a falsehood, which are inextricably interlocked in one's emotions. If one takes it as it is and forms it with one's senses, giving it the shape of reality, what arises is dreams and art; but between these two and real, full life there is a glass wall.

Throughout *The Man Without Qualities*, Musil includes several passages in which he tries to map out his own relationship to metaphor. In one very long passage, he describes the role of metaphors at different stages of growing up and entering young adulthood. Here, he sees metaphor as a continual attempt to escape the confinements of language.

The excessive use of metaphor can be dangerous, and this is assuming the metaphors are good to begin with. By 'good' I mean effective in breaking the circuitry of bureaucracy and control inherent in the common currency of words. Metaphors are indulgent exactly because, to build on Musil's thoughts, they serve the author's personal drive for emancipation, which doesn't necessarily translate as such to the reader.

But the time I'm writing in is very different from Musil's. He wrote his epic trilogy in Vienna and Switzerland between the two World Wars. In his world, a glass wall was still deeply material. Sheet glass, the technological innovation that radically altered the possibilities for glass architecture, had been invented not long before. Musil could never have imagined the glass skyscrapers littering the globe's capitals or what it feels like to go through airports shrouded in the maximum security of transparency, or what if feels like to spend most of one's waking hours staring into an illuminated pane of glass that mediates the largest accumulation of knowledge ever dreamt of.

The ability to describe a hard material boundary made of

glass doesn't quite resonate in my time. While glass is still clearly a material, its application is in many ways liquid and narrative. It is widely used to signify ideological narratives that are mostly false. The banks that occupy skyscrapers aren't in fact transparent operations. The glass with which they're constructed has more to say about the liquidity of global financial structures than about anything one could see inside their walls.

Musil's metaphors rely on the presumed stability of an inside and an outside, a definition that has always been tenuous if not imaginary. But as historically imagined boundaries increasingly dissolve in the contemporary consciousness the ability to discern a metaphor from a literal description of a thing, state or feeling also becomes increasingly undefined. Language often performs a series of manoeuvres by which it describes the function of a symbolic ideal, while denying the reality of how it is experienced. In some cases, metaphors are necessary simply to describe what is there and rescue experience from what it has been instrumentalized to signify. Dreams (or nightmares) and art (and artifice) are so thoroughly interwoven into the fabric of 'real, full life' that the word *real* itself can only ever function at an ironic remove.

Because I spent my childhood moving between different countries, pop culture was perhaps the only constant in all of the radically different environments I found myself in. It was the one currency I could exchange no matter where I was. Pop's signal has a unifying power that is often much stronger than political policies and actions. It crosses national and linguistic barriers through shear force. People sing whole songs over and over without ever understanding the lyrics, and yet it speaks to them.

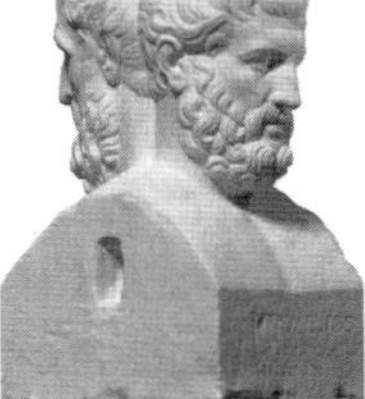

Pop has a weird relationship to metaphor. Pop stars are at once real people who exist in the physical world and empty vessels for projection caught in a virtual

　　THE MIRACLE-INDUSTRIAL COMPLEX

abstraction. The lyrics they broadcast often refer to their own selves literally but simultaneously become vehicles for feeling templates that any listener can use as means of expression. Pop is powerful because it is embodied in its listeners; it speaks at and for listeners at the same time. In that sense it is neither internal nor external. It is at once literal and metaphorical. Reading into the nuances found in pop culture sometimes sheds light on profound and un-expected cultural truths, often inaccessible through other means. But potential truth evaporates into meaninglessness the moment it is taken literally.

Here, the part truth, part falsehood of Musil's glass bound-ary is entangled in ways that deny real separations. Pop *is* the glass wall or maybe better, the prism emitted by a piece of glass refracting light from a specific angle. Pop is never situated on one side or the other; the personal is performed and the performance is personalized.

In a culture shaped by a level of scientific determinism, the void left by the absence of mythical beings, deities, mira-cles and spirits in active belief structures has in many ways been replaced by pop culture. The public follows celebrities in real time and is educated in a complex and massive reference framework that has outgrown the scale of Greek mythology, for example, many times over. This ever-growing and evolving framework is full of super-heroes and villains, angels and devils, monsters, creatures and aliens. It produces tragedies and miracles, downfalls and rebirths. It is deeply entangled in the hollowed-out (but still forceful) shell of Christianity, while also allowing the space for pagan and animist forms of worship. All of these activities produce a raw energy that oscillates between the literal and the metaphorical.

> It is not self-evident what one is thinking about when the topic is energy. Like the notions of force, will, work, and the sacred, energy seems to name at the same time something internal, immaterial, and spiritual and something material, concrete, and physical. [EE]

In retrospect, the 1990s were a time of unprecedented miracles. The globe had just been cracked open and capital was free to shine its messianic light onto regions previously shrouded in darkness. A common currency was granted the power not only to create a universal measure for all commodities, but also to measure all life on the planet and beyond. Language, ritual, identity and heritage all had a role to play in this currency, their respective values calibrated to unlock their maximum affective powers. War, as history had recorded it, and as people knew to recognize it, was almost entirely replaced with the more rational pursuit of profit. The scope of this unifying project was nothing short of miraculous. It would have been inconceivable without the guiding strength of higher (or lower) powers. In 1998 God became a DJ, but in the first half of the decade he moved heaven and earth.

I feel that I experienced a small part of this miraculous era first-hand. My mother, a Jewish American, met my German father in West Berlin, which was at the time a walled-off island on the Soviet side of the Iron Curtain. They got married, my father converted to Judaism, and I was born in 1985. For several years they performed the role of a progressive Jewish family well enough to convince me that I was Jewish. I liked God. I talked to Him frequently.

In 1988, we moved from West Berlin to New Haven, Connecticut, so that my mother could assume a position as a professor at Yale University. Our first year there we lived in the ghetto. My father, the German alien who spoke only rudimentary English, would observe everything around him tirelessly. American culture must have appeared insane to him. I think he often lacked the ability to avert his gaze from the flamboyance that enveloped and intoxicated him. Late one afternoon, he was standing at our window, gawking at the neighbours on the street, who happened to be selling drugs. They shot at him and the bullet flew by his ear

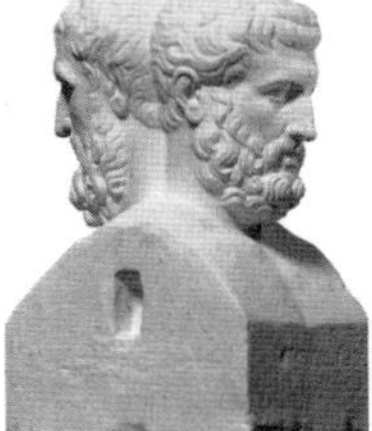

                       THE MIRACLE-INDUSTRIAL COMPLEX

and lodged itself into the wall above the bed where I, four years old, was taking a nap.

After this incident, we moved to an apartment directly on the Yale University campus, an elite enclave then still nestled into the ghettos that surrounded it on three sides. In one of my earliest memories, the three of us are sitting in the living room of that apartment one autumn evening. We

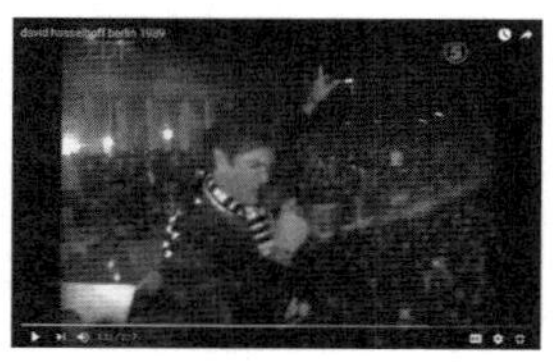

hear students outside yelling: *'The Cold War is over!'* My parents rush to turn on the TV and watch in disbelief as a sea of East Berliners storm through the checkpoints that had defined the parameters of their previous lives.

My mother booked tickets for the first available flight, and within a couple of days the three of us were at the Berlin Wall, picks in hand, happily chipping away at oppression. For weeks, Berliners from East and West gathered with friends and families to break small pieces off the wall. It was something of a recreational activity. I remember this labour being incredibly difficult. None of us could really do much damage to the reinforced concrete with the picks we had purchased for the occasion. We resolved to pick up graffiti covered pieces of debris that were lying on the ground. My mother stuffed them in a bag, certain this rubble would be worth a fortune in a future without walls. When we returned to New Haven a week or so later, she distributed little pieces to her friends as souvenirs.

I always loved watching TV, and I loved *MTV* in particular,

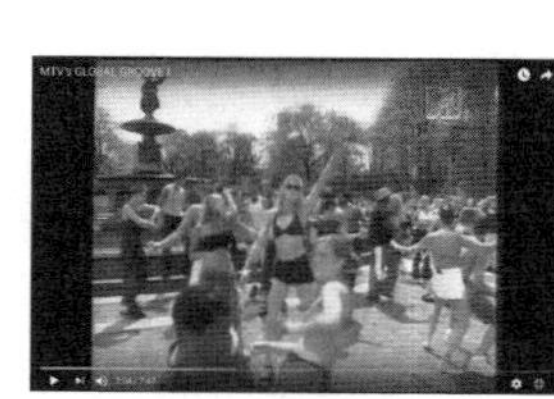

with a passion I've rarely had for much else. My mother, the sole breadwinner in the family, had strict rules about how much TV I was allowed to watch. My father, an unemployed alcoholic, would be in charge of looking after my younger sisters and I when my mother was gone. We would sit together, me around seven years old, my father usually under the influence of a dangerous cocktail of antipsychotics and alcohol, and watch shows like *MTV Grind* and *Global Groove*.

Global Groove, with its interactive interface, which

straddled the media shift from TV to the Internet, was one of the many miracles that were part of shaping this unifying time. The interface had a grid showing four different locations across the globe from London to Tokyo to New York, while a stream of half-naked bodies in unimaginably distant places competed for the camera's attention. We'd watch this post-racial celebration of sexy young bodies dancing to songs like: *all I wanna do is zoom a zoom zoom zoom and a boom boom—just shake yo rump.*

My father, who, as I mentioned, struggled with basic English, must have been fascinated by this new language emerging in rap, a language that pushed an aggressive assertion of otherness, while also being all the mainstream rage—a language that broke the grammar rules he would never comprehend himself. He somehow never came to terms with the English word *fart*, stuck as he was on the German word *furz.* Trying to speak English, he'd say something like *fartz or fertz.* I remember this being unbearably embarrassing to me on several occasions.

In the realm of miracles, I've started to think of representation as something like a certificate of authenticity. Something abnormal occurs: an encounter with a spirit, a UFO, the delicate after-image of Christ on a piece of cloth. From the perspective of power, these extraordinary subjective moments are necessary because they contain in themselves a level of perceived freedom. But that freedom is precarious: it has the potential to question the veil of objectivity necessary to maintain power. Power constantly adapts itself so it can find adequate forms for such ambiguous experience and thereby defines what margins of formless subjectivity can be tolerated without losing control. It is this cultural infrastructure I choose to call the miracle-industrial complex.

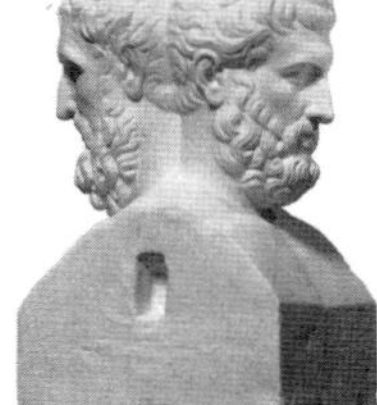

The miracle-industrial complex is an infrastructure of extraction operating in tandem with the extraction of energy and materials used to fuel the economic and military operations on which it is built. While the military-industrial complex extracts the earth's resources, the miracle-industrial complex extracts affect, identity, and memories from people, converting that abstract amorphous energy into quantifiable and certifiable proofs of authenticity. A collective consciousness is formed on the faulty foundations of metaphors taken to be literal.

America in the early nineties took the issuing of such certificates of authenticity to an unprecedented industrial scale, producing representations of miracles at the rate of a nation printing money to stave off financial collapse. As several histories will attest, this type of currency inflation never ends well, but first I'm just interested in describing some features of this surplus.

> In the 1990s, angels, it seemed, were everywhere... *Angelos* means messenger in Greek, and angels have traditionally been considered luminescent agents of the Logos, figures of order, communication, and knowledge. Manifesting the helpful side of Hermes, angels mediate between an inaccessible but omniscient godhead and the earthly spheres where humans lumber along in the dark. So perhaps it is no accident that these mediators return in our datapocalyptic days, for they form blazing icons of the only faith that many people now hold: that information and communication will somehow save us. [TG]

One of the miracles being represented on an industrial scale in the nineties was the message that racism was over. This was the belief that shaped the environment of my childhood, both at home and in the external world as it entered my young consciousness. This was what my mother, having grown up in the American South during the civil-rights era, believed to be true.

The airwaves were full of pop songs begging people for

compassion: for neighbours, for strangers, for the Other. Suffering was made quantifiable. The cure was within rational reach. For a single dollar a day you could change someone's life. The commodities you had outworn or no longer desired could be sent around the globe and accepted as gifts. Guilt turned to vindication. The past, whether in the form of colonial atrocities or old clothes you'd worn out, could somehow be forgotten and everyone could move on to better things together.

> Inauthenticity operates as complicity with anonymous materials. [CP]

Every push to hear myself is a battle against the more powerful signals that beg for my attention. Pop is too powerful and too sincere, and everything else is less than simulation. The thin layer of my containment is too weak. I have to work within the fractured flow of inattention. I've been trying to train myself to think through distraction, with distraction.

I miss you like the deserts miss the rain. I wanna fuck you (make love?) like the rain fucks the desert, like the rain swallows grains of dry sand to make globs of something dangerously unknown: decay. I miss you like something I've never known. But the feeling of missing you (who?—you) remains. I don't know the desert and the desert doesn't know the rain. If it did its hole identity would evaporate whole. My heart has the power to move ecosystems. My heart has the power to invent a past in which deserts knew rain but I still miss you (who?) now. I don't know. I can't remember.

> The inability to remember is usually associated with the paralytic symptoms of memory holes; in this case, the subject is not able to access the memory. If memory holes cause such accessibility problems

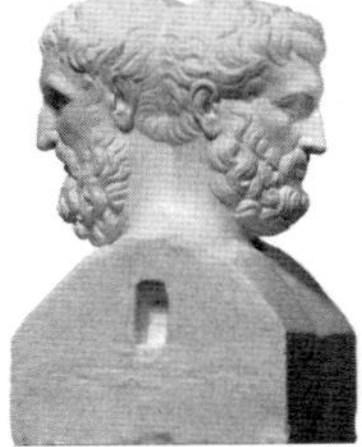

THE MIRACLE-INDUSTRIAL COMPLEX

for the subject, it is because they have been specifically designed for being accessed from the other side. In this sense, memory holes are accessible not for the subject and its integrated self but for that which is exterior to the subject and has no self (no one). If remembering is unrealistic and futile in terms of memory holes, then inversely memory holes are gates and access points; they conduct remembering and other modes of access toward a memory which belongs to the outside. [CP]

By creating a new interface between the self, the other, and the world beyond, media technologies become *part* of the self, the other, and the world beyond. [TG]

The Cold War and the iron curtain symbolized the greatest socio-political and psychological divide in history. By the early nineties—that miraculous time—the rubble had been cleared away; there were no more man-made boundaries of that scale to stand in the way of unlimited growth. Throughout history, heartbreak had often projected itself onto man-made structures. In the nineties, heartbreak turned to ecologies, now theoretically accessible from any point on the globe within hours. Heartbreak has always been a resource of immense energy, but now it was capable of shifting whole landscapes and transplanting entire ecosystems.

The American boy band Boyz II Men played a sizeable role in the miracle-industrial complex. Like many of their peers, they used awards shows to thank their Christian God directly. The transition from boy to man implied in their name might channel the rites of passage into adulthood that have defined almost every social body in history, now wrapped in the gloss of global pop. But in their case, they performed something more subtle and profound. Their rite of passage was also racial, a powerful transformation by which the demeaning *boy* was finally allowed to become a man. *Boyz*, the Ebonics Z, was then still tethered to the representation of black culture.

The Boyz II Men song, *Four Seasons of Loneliness* (1997), is about an unresolved love drenched in melancholy nostalgia: *I long for, the warmth of, days gone by.* A song about seasons, the video represents each of the four literally, matching (conveniently) each of the group's four singers. But in the metaphorical abstraction of the video, the seasons change in a void of time and space. Each of the singers is hurled through the cosmos to land in a different ecosystem: the white North Pole, a green jungle, an autumnal forest in orange, and a deserted beach. In each ecosystem, a lover, dressed appropriately for the season, awaits the landing of one of the four.

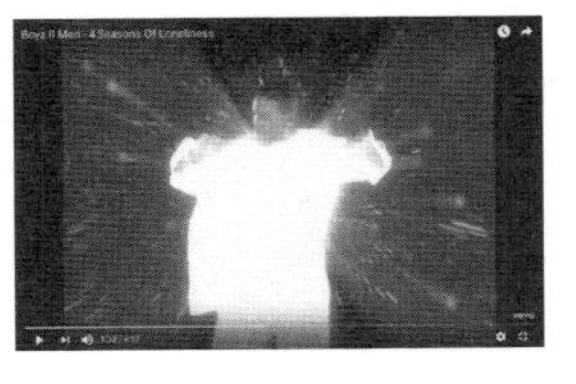

> In both the popular and the technocratic imagination, information and its technologies began to take on an almost redemptive character as they battled noise and error—the communications equivalent of dissipation and decay. [TG]

The video could be seen as a manual for broadcast mediation in the miracle-industrial-complex. The signal of purity travels at the speed of light. It is unconstrained by geographical boundaries, nation states, by race or language. The signal comes from the pure white of nowhere and arrives as love in the colourful everywhere. It touches down in landscapes devoid of inhabitants and lingers in the purity of a love lost. The purity of the message is prone to noise and distortion. The video employs several glitch filters as well as other optical devices to show the distortion inherent in transmission. The apparatus requires constant upkeep and system updates. Christianity can host different bodies but the purity of its disembodied spirit must be maintained.

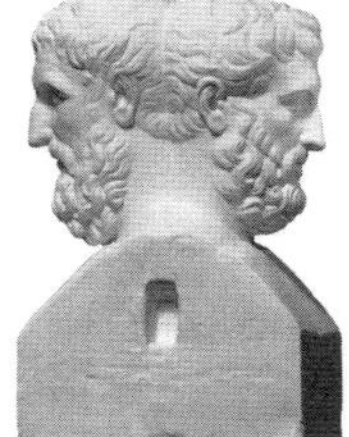

As (cyberlibertarian) John Perry Barlow forcefully put it in a post

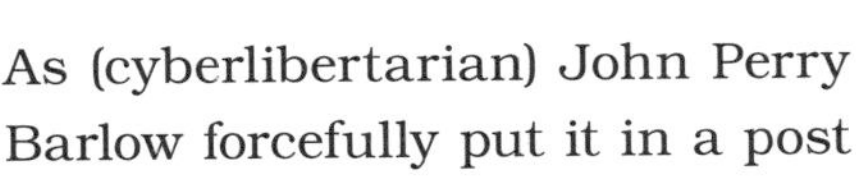

     THE MIRACLE-INDUSTRIAL COMPLEX

to the Nettime mailing list (1996): Nature is itself a free market system. A rain forest is an unplanned economy, as is a coral reef. The difference between an economy that sorts the information and energy in photons and one that sorts the information and energy in dollars is a slight one in my mind. Economy is ecology. [TG]

In 1993, the English band Everything But The Girl released their song *Missing*. It wasn't until Todd Terry made a dance remix of it in 1994 that the song became a global hit, covered widely by artists like such as Sade, for example, to

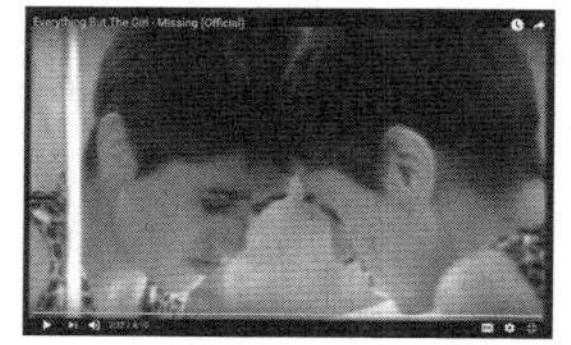

broadcast the iconic line *I miss you like the deserts miss the rain*. This was a message that already acknowledged, albeit subconsciously, the technology used to broadcast this message to be an ecosystem complex enough to parallel the ecologies it projected itself onto. In retrospect, it seems to illustrate a profound perceptual shift that had, in just a short time, come to reconfigure the relationship of the human to the natural world.

For the desert to miss the rain, the desert's entire identity as an ecosystem would be forced to change, for a desert is a desert precisely because it doesn't rain. While masked in the individuality of heartbreak, this newly forming (sub)consciousness was being narrated autonomously. The angels of communication technologies sang of ideological purity, while the energy extraction needed to unify distant geographical locations was, in the process, altering those ecosystems irrevocably.

In *Cyclonopedia*, Reza Negarestani describes oil as a narrator, one that collects the microcosms found in each grain of sand to distribute its narrative throughout its activities as a planetary entity.

Each particle carries crystallized waste matter and essences of different groups and particularities, hard

AUTHENTICITY?

to grasp but easy to commingle with fluid. … this fluid or wetness, essential for blending the dust particles in the Middle East into one narrative with multiple undertows, is petroleum, or *napht* (oil). In the Avesta language of ancient Persia, the word napht is the word for wetness itself. [CP]

Bringing rain to the desert creates wetness, but not a cleansing wetness; this is a sticky, unruly, decaying wetness. Today the wetness of ecological disaster feels remarkably like the blindness of heartbreak, like the feeling of yearning for something imagined, never actually experienced, but symbolically strong in its internalized abstraction. The extraction of oil enacts the dual process of unification by dissolving distance and turning proximity alien. It seems logical that this would be felt most strongly in the heart where reason and logic break down into blind emotion.

Negarestani also proposes the idea that oil, a planetary entity endowed with its own consciousness was waiting for humans to arrive and begin its extraction.

[T]ake Oil as a lubricant, something that eases narration and the whole dynamism toward the desert. The cartography of oil as an omnipresent entity narrates the dynamics of planetary events. Oil is the undercurrent of all narrations, not only the political but also that of the ethics of life on earth. [CP]

Sometimes the snow comes down in June
Sometimes the sun goes round the moon
I see the passion in your eyes
Sometimes it's all a big surprise[1]

1
Vanessa Williams, *Save The Best For Last*, 1991, The Island Def Jam Music Group

Looking back at the record left by the miracle-industrial complex, I observe how the quest for purity pursued outside physical space and time had

　　　　　　　THE MIRACLE-INDUSTRIAL COMPLEX

disastrous effects. Maybe the angels already intuited this. They sang of loneliness and alienation at a time when there was excessive surplus of everything. Maybe they sensed that ecosystems couldn't be transplanted without that transformation leading to all kinds of unexpected mutations.

In 2016, a couple of weeks after Donald Trump was elected president of the United States, I watched a live VH1 performance from 1995 featuring Boyz II Men singing their song *Heal The World*. Halfway through the performance a burst of light blinds the camera filming the performance, and Michael Jackson emerges from the halo to sing his *We Are The World*. How was it that while boyz were in the process of becoming men, Michael Jackson had already become white? *I miss you like the deserts miss the rain.*

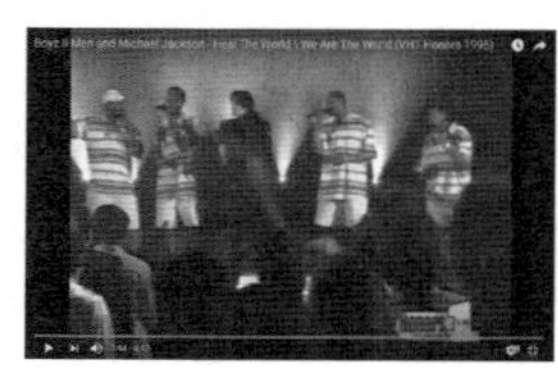

The severance of landscapes from their images wasn't something that happened in some remote, inaccessible landscape. It happened in the very composition of our own consciousness. In parallel to the detachment landscapes would undergo, race, religion and heritage would be recalculated according to an affective visual marketplace, in some distant miraculous sphere beyond experience. These processes of detachment and relocation have happened throughout time in different shapes and forms, but never on this quantifiable, industrialized scale. While the split between one's image and presumed self is obvious in the age of social media, these tools weren't catalysts but symptoms of long term processes. In a sense, social media delivered a message that came late, and then only on false terms.

As the self is extracted and refined into marketable affect, individual consciousness is replaced by a vast infrastructure in which personal experience is little more than fuel needed to maintain appearances. Personal memories become impossible to separate from the world events that determined their parameters.

There is a famous interview with Michael Jackson where he insists he never changed his skin colour. He says his skin change was the result of a skin condition that slowly started turning his skin white over time. The interviewer later brings this up with his long-time make-up artist and friend. She confirms that for a long time, she had to cover emerging white spots with make-up in darker colours to look consistent. At a certain point the white spots had outgrown the dark spots so they just decided to cover the dark spots instead. The whole claim is so uncanny, as are the circumstances that produced him. I watch this document almost twenty years later and find myself desperately wanting to believe them. I can't determine where the memory gap is; with me, with him, or with the metaphorical reality that he had no choice but to call his own.

From a recent email exchange:

```
Subject: I wonder what you think of this

   hey ma,

   i finished writing the first draft of this
   longer essay which i just sent to the editor.

   aside from wanting to share and wanting
   to hear your thoughts, it has some
   autobiographical passages. there are some
   initially disparate things i put together or
   theatricalized for the sake of what i thought
   would make a better story. but i'm curious
   to see if you think any of it is wrong or
   really misremembered.

   love,
   b
```

   THE MIRACLE-INDUSTRIAL COMPLEX

Re: I wonder what you think of this

hey beny,

i think this essay is excellent.

you asked about misremembering. it was quite
weird reading the autobiographical parts
because you did misremember, on the other
hand they make a good and coherent story so
i'm not exactly suggesting that you change
anything. but just fyi: we lived on the edge
of the ghetto, not in the ghetto (i wouldn't
have been that careless) and yes your father
was gawking at the people on the street but
it was nighttime, not afternoon, and you
were three not four. as for 9 november–nice
that it's one of your first memories. but the
television didn't work so your father and i
went to a bar; i don't think we took you with
us, so where were you? i am certain that the
tv wasn't working so we went to a bar because
the barman was amazed that we wanted to
watch the news instead of the football game
and when we said we were from berlin, he let
us watch for a bit and then said 'ok, you're
free now, can we go back to the game, adolf?'
tja… i also didn't book the next available
flight because i had a job, so had to wait
till the semester was over but did book the
first flight for that. and you are certainly
right that it was almost impossible to get
a chip out of the fucking wall, really hard.

but as i said your version does work
dramatically so it's not clear that you
should change anything. you'll have to decide

about the role of truth in autobiography...
and i liked your extension of our email
correspondence.

love,
ma

Reference Codes
TG Erik Davis, *TechGnosis: Myth, Magic, and Mysticism
in the Age of Information* (Berkeley, CA, 2015).
EE Antti Salminen and Tere Vadén, *Energy and Experience:
An Essay in Nafthology* (Chicago, 2015).
CP Reza Negarestani, *Cyclonopedia: Complicity with
Anonymous Materials (Anomaly)* (Melbourne, 2008).

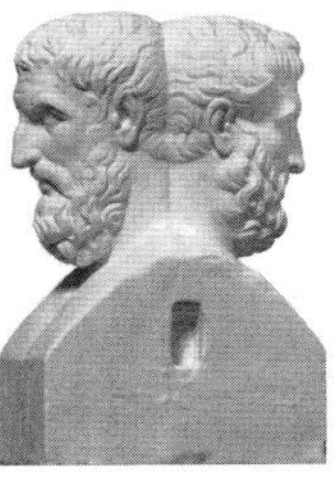

 THE MIRACLE-INDUSTRIAL COMPLEX

IMAGE EXPLOSION

David Joselit

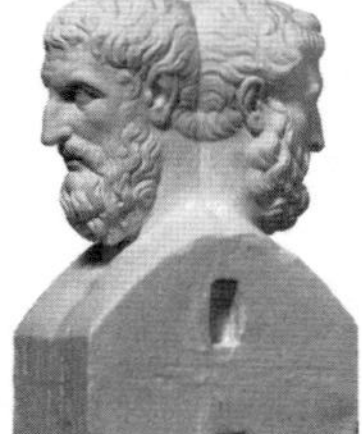

1

See James Gleick, *The Information: A History; a Theory; a Flood* (New York, 2011).

2

Carol Vogel, 'The Buzz in Basel: Art, Alive and Well and Selling Briskly', *New York Times*, 17 June 2010.

The scale at which images proliferate and the speed at which they travel have never been greater.[1] Under these conditions, images appear to be free, but they carry a price. Commenting to the *New York Times* on the 2010 edition of Art Basel, the world's most prestigious modern and contemporary art fair, American collector Donald Rubell declared, with no apparent irony, 'People are now realizing that art is an international currency'.[2] (The new museums designed for cities around the world by star architects such as Frank Gehry, Renzo Piano, Jacques Herzog, and Pierre de Meuron would thus function as the art world's central banks.) In a time of economic instability that has been precipitated by worldwide financial failures since 2008, people see art as an international currency. It is a fungible hedge whose value (at least when it is sold at fairs such as Art Basel, in prestigious auction houses, and at blue-chip galleries throughout the world) must cross borders as easily as the dollar, the euro, the yen, and the renminbi. By definition, a currency moves freely (though not at no cost). It is an instrument invented to transfer value easily and efficiently—and now, with the aid of computers, almost instantaneously. Even the negligible materiality of paper money has grown practically obsolete, and is required only for a fraction of transactions. Currencies are universal translators: they can assign a value to commodities of every kind, whether goods or services. In the 1990s, a second type of universal translator gained prominence: digital technologies with the capacity to transpose any work in sound, image, or text into numerical sequences—that is, into code. Contemporary art and architecture are produced at the intersection of these two universal translators—one specifying value; the other, format. But how can we describe the aesthetics of a currency such as art?

First, we must discard the concept of the medium (along with its mirror image, the postmedium), which has been fundamental to art history and criticism for generations.

This category privileges discrete objects—even those that are attenuated, mute, distributed, or 'dematerialized'. One of the goals of *After Art* is to expand the definition of art to embrace heterogeneous configurations of relationships or links—what the French artist Pierre Huyghe has called 'a dynamic chain that passes through different formats'.[3] Medium and postmedium are not good analytical tools for describing the hybridity of such chains or 'currencies' of different formats. Here we may take a lesson from late-capitalist business practices, according to which virtually anything, from trash to home mortgages, may be 'monetized'—in other words, exchanged on an international market in an abstracted representational form. Rubell maintains that art has been monetized, too—as a universal currency. This has unfortunately resulted in vast commercialization, but it has also vested images with an enhanced form of power, which *After Art* is dedicated to exploring.

Our first task in assessing what kind of currency art might be, or become, is to understand the dynamics of its circulation, since, by definition, currencies are constituted through exchange. At the moment, there are two dominant attitudes vis-à-vis the circulation of art. Not coincidentally, they each correspond to those that structure contemporary global politics. The first is aligned to the world of Art Basel, and to most large Western museums: it is a belief in the free 'neoliberal' circulation of images, whereby open markets turn art (as well as other streams of images from a range of sources, all the way from television to tweets) into a form of currency.

The second attitude might be described as fundamentalist: it posits that art and architecture are rooted to a specific place.[4] Religious fundamentalism is defined by adherence to a doctrine that is laid down in sacred texts. Image fundamentalism asserts that a visual

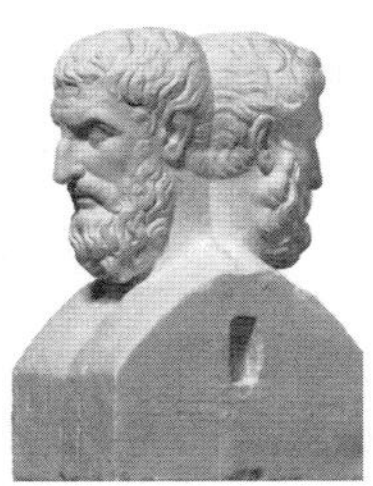

3
This is a description by the artist Pierre Huyghe of his own model of objectivity, which I think could be expanded to encompass the nature of contemporary images *tout court*. George Baker, 'An Interview with Pierre Huyghe', *October* 110 (Fall 2004), pp. 80–106, p. 90.

4
For a different perspective on these issues, see Sven Lütticken, *Idols of the Market: Modern Iconoclasm and the Fundamentalist Spectacle* (Berlin, 2009).

IMAGE EXPLOSION

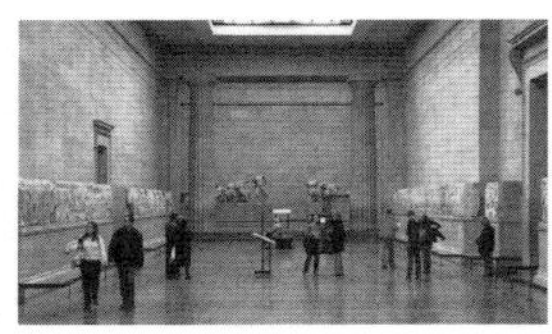

Figure 1
Elgin (Parthenon) Marbles installed at the British Museum, London.

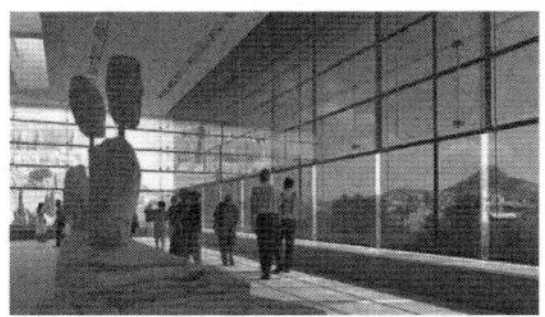

Figure 2
Bernard Tschumi, architect, Acropolis Museum, Athens. Installation shot of top gallery, showing where the Elgin (Parthenon) Marbles would be installed were they returned.

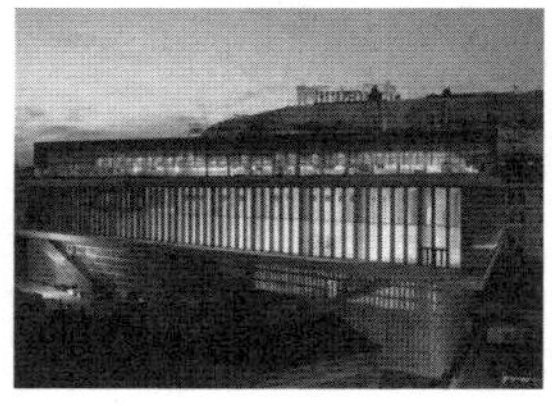

Figure 3
Bernard Tschumi, architect, Acropolis Museum, overall view of front of building at dusk.

artefact belongs exclusively to a specific site (its place of origin). It insists, for instance, that the Parthenon sculptures sold to the British Museum in 1816 by Thomas Bruce, Seventh Earl of Elgin (fig. 1), who removed them from the Acropolis with the permission of the Ottoman Empire—the legality of whose decision has subsequently been vigorously questioned—should be returned to Bernard Tschumi's state-of-the-art Acropolis Museum, which was built especially to draw these works back to Athens (figs. 2 and 3), and which opened in 2008.

It is worth pausing to assert that this great political conflict—between neoliberalism and the fundamentalisms that have emerged in both the developed and developing worlds, and that encompass most major religions, including Christianity, Judaism, Islam, and Hinduism—is not merely reflected in, but advanced by, art. Art has a diplomatic portfolio: it participates in the building of new public spheres and in the opening of export markets abroad. Since 1979, to take one prominent example, Chinese contemporary art has been closely aligned, in how it has been exhibited, with the ups and downs of domestic political liberalization—a practice that the artist Ai Weiwei has adapted to the Internet by, for instance, publishing on his blog troubling revelations about the tragic deaths of schoolchildren in poorly built schools in the great Sichuan earthquake of 2008.[5] It may seem that the Chinese art world's enthusiastic embrace of the art market disqualifies that world as a political force, but in his provocative book *The Party and the Arty in China: The New Politics of Culture* (2004), political scientist Richard Curt Kraus argues the opposite: that the success of Chinese artists in the international art market has led to a relaxing of restrictions in the cultural realm and consequently greater political openness overall:

Despite the violence of the 1989 Beijing Massacre, political reform in China has been more profound

AUTHENTICITY?

5

The art historian Wu Hung has argued that exhibitions are central to an understanding of contemporary Chinese art through their capacity to open small, temporary, but often virulent public spheres where an intellectual and artistic vanguard can incrementally broaden the scope of artistic freedom as well as of political speech in China. See, e.g., Wu Hung, *Transience: Chinese Experimental Art at the End of the Twentieth Century*, rev. ed. David and Alfred Smart Museum of Art (Chicago, 2005); and the 'Exhibition Section' of Wu Hung, *Making History* (Hong Kong, 2008), pp. 157–215.

6

Richard Curt Kraus, *The Party and the Arty in China: The New Politics of Culture* (Lanham, Md., 2004), p. 28.

7

Indeed, I may be overemphasizing differences here, where similarities are more significant. Many of the historical avant-gardes— including, for instance, Dada, the Bauhaus, De Stijl, and Surrealism—were committed to an international effort to produce new forms of public perception and political action.

8

One might add identity politics and media strategies as equally international styles, but I would argue that these may also be placed in the genealogy of Conceptual Art.

than is commonly recognized: artists (and other intellectuals) have established a new more autonomous relationship with the state. The price of this growing independence is financial insecurity, commercial vulgarization, and the specter of unemployment.[6]

Given the crackdowns on dissident Chinese intellectuals after the public protests during the Arab Spring in 2011—including Ai's detention for eighty- one days for alleged economic crimes—Kraus's optimism may seem misplaced. However, it is clear that Ai's international reputation led to pressure on the Chinese to release him, including representations made by German Foreign Minister Guido Westerwelle. If art has political efficacy in the twenty-first century, it may lie in cultural diplomacy as opposed to the invention of avant-garde forms (fig. 4).[7]

The debates surrounding the repatriation of cultural property in the first decade of the twenty-first century are a very different sort of diplomatic dilemma. Though not fought over works of contemporary art, these controversies nonetheless constitute a thoroughly contemporary conflict between a neoliberal model of free circulation and a fundamentalist belief that art belongs to a unique place. Indeed, like Conceptual Art—the most widespread 'international style' to emerge since the mid-1960s—the contemporary ethics of cultural property hinge on information.[8] In response to a thriving trade in illicit antiquities, whose original archaeological context is typically undocumented, in 1970 UNESCO Member States agreed an international treaty, the Convention on the Means of Prohibiting and Preventing the Illicit Import, Export and Transport of Ownership of Cultural Property. The Convention posits a clear theory of value that can be applied to archaeological artefacts:

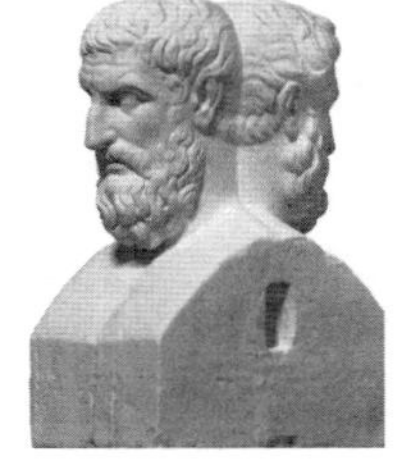

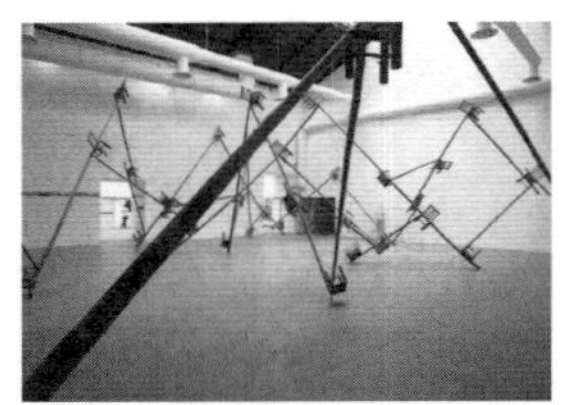

Figure 4
Ai Weiwei, *Installation Piece for Venice Biennale* (in collaboration with Herzog & de Meuron), 2008. Bamboo wood, 236.2 × 393.7 × 275.6 in. (600 × 1,000 × 700 cm).

> [C]ultural property constitutes one of the basic elements of civilization and national culture, and … its true value can be appreciated only in relation to the fullest possible information regarding its origin.

It is not only that the Convention holds that informational value is 'truer' than aesthetic value (and in the same year as two watershed exhibitions of Conceptual Art in New York, 'Information' at the Museum of Modern Art, and 'Software' at the Jewish Museum, also sought to redefine the work of art as a form of information). It is also that enforcement of the Convention relies on a second genre of information: the thorough documentation of an object's 'history'—a continuous chain of custody that can authenticate its provenance.

These repatriation debates took centre stage in the first decade of the twenty-first century. That decade also witnessed legal actions such as Italy's prosecution of former Getty Museum curator Marion True for acquiring illegally exported antiquities, as well as the opening of the new Acropolis Museum as part of the Greek government's effort to persuade Great Britain to return the so-called Elgin Marbles (not to mention many less-well-publicized scandals and campaigns). That this was so makes sense, because what is at stake are the ethical—and even moral—dilemmas that arise when cultural properties are virtually freed from the limits of space and time. Should images flow freely like currencies, anywhere the market will take them, or should this neoliberal freedom be tempered by the values of cultural identity whose most extreme expression is fundamentalist? Indeed, the repatriation debates allow us to distinguish three objects, each constituting its own paradigm of cultural circulation—the migrant object, the native object, and the documented object—each of which possesses its own relationship to a site of origin, its own form of value, and its own particular legal status, in terms that recall one of the most charged political issues

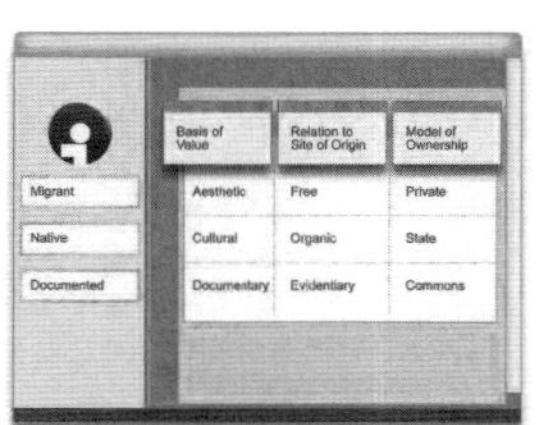

Diagram 1
Designed by Geoff Kaplan.

of our time—illegal immigration among migrant laborers, and massive flows of refugees from war-ravaged parts of the developing world (diagram 1).

The migrant object's site of origin may be unclear, but its history can gradually acquire a patina of legitimacy as it is passed along a chain of owners: galleries, prominent collectors, and, ultimately, museums. Its cultural value lies in its aesthetic power, but legally it is owned as a commodity—and the sovereign authority of property rights may be used to mask illegitimate claims about its provenance. The 'information' carried by migrant objects is believed to be inherent in their form rather than dependent upon their site of origin. In a controversial book published in 2008, *Who Owns Antiquity?: Museums and the Battle over Our Ancient Heritage*, the current CEO of the Getty Trust in Los Angeles, James Cuno, recounts his first visit to the Louvre as a college student:

> I was not the lesser for not being 'from' these magnificent cultures. They were not inaccessible to me, though in many cases I had never heard of them and in every case knew little if anything about them. They were not foreign, in the sense of being of another's culture. They were mine, too. Or, rather, I was theirs. … And I looked at them in wonder, too; in ways, I imagined, their original beholders looked at them.[9]

9
James Cuno, *Who Owns Antiquity?: Museums and the Battle over Our Ancient Heritage* (Princeton, 2008), pp. 156–157.

As Cuno's treacly account makes clear, with the 'migrant object', the right of possession depends neither on cultural commonality nor on special knowledge, but rather on pure empathy. Consequently, its relation to its original site may easily be severed so that it can be released into free and unfettered markets. The native object, by contrast, belongs organically to a specific place. While it may be of the highest aesthetic quality, its primary value is tied to a specific cultural identity, and typically it belongs—or is

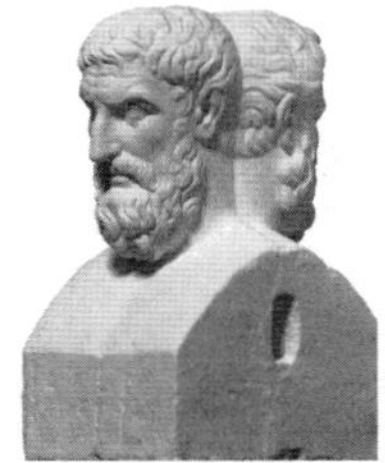

said to belong—to the state. Melina Mercouri, who was the Greek Minister of Culture and Sciences when Greece began its efforts to repatriate the Parthenon Marbles, declared in an address to the Oxford Union in 1986:

> You must understand what the Parthenon Marbles mean to us. They are our pride. They are our sacrifices. They are our noblest symbol of excellence. They are a tribute to the democratic philosophy. They are our aspirations and our name. They are the essence of Greekness.[10]

Native objects are absolutely site-specific: if displaced, they are said to be maimed—rendered meaningless.

Finally, there is the documented object, whose relationship to its original site or 'find spot' (which is technically known as a provenience) has been properly studied to produce for the object an informational or documentary value. Even if such an object is removed from its place of origin and acquired by a collection on the other side of the world, the knowledge that is derived from it—and that it represents from then on—becomes part of the cultural commons. For archaeologist John Carman, access to knowledge of this kind is a necessary but not a sufficient public good. In his book *Against Cultural Property: Archaeology, Heritage and Ownership*, Carman rejects the ownership of cultural property in any form—whether by a nation state or a museum—as inherently reducing material culture to nothing more than an economic asset that must be exploited:

> This brings us finally to the core but unstated notion which sustains all of the value structures of the economic approach but which ultimately denies the ubiquity of the environment: that value only accrues to things that are in some sense, and in some way, owned.[11]

10
Address by Melina Mercouri, Minister of Culture and Sciences of Greece to the Oxford Union, 12 June 1986, `http://webcache.googleusercontent.com/search?q=cache:iSRY17mCgrQJ:melinamercourifoundation.com/en/the-parthenon-marbles/the-parhenon-marbles/+&cd=3&hl=nl&ct=clnk&gl=nl`.

11
John Carman, *Against Cultural Property: Archaeology, Heritage and Ownership* (London, 2005), p. 73.

Carman advocates instead community management of cultural heritage. As utopian as this position may sound, it is salutary to imagine how material culture, and image cultures of all descriptions, could be valued other than as property. Images might become forms of currency that, like many forms of communication, do not conform to the monetary.[12] Because they emerge in an information era in which documentation is virtually inherent to the production of art, contemporary artworks typically belong to the category of documented objects. The question of art's circulation or currency—whether the object in question is migrant, native, or documented—is thus intricately bound up with various understandings of its site-specificity. It was Walter Benjamin who offered the most compelling theorizations around twentieth-century mechanical reproduction, and who has also produced the most enduring model of how art belongs to a place. Indeed, in his famous essay *The Work of Art in the Age of Its Technological Reproducibility*, the dialectic I have identified between the 'native' and the 'neoliberal' is already encoded. (Perhaps that is why his influential theorization of art's site-specificity in terms of aura is cited as widely and as compulsively today as when it entered the Anglo-American canon of the postmodern 1980s. But Benjamin's essay can hardly account for the revolutions in image production and circulation initiated by media such as television, the Internet, and mobile phones since its publication in the mid-1930s. His brilliant analysis has become a roadblock.

This problem is caused, not by Benjamin's failure, but by our own. There is still no better analysis than his of the economic-aesthetic 'regime change' that occurs when mechanical reproduction causes the unit of aesthetic analysis to shift from individual works to virtually unlimited populations of images. But in order to value the art of our

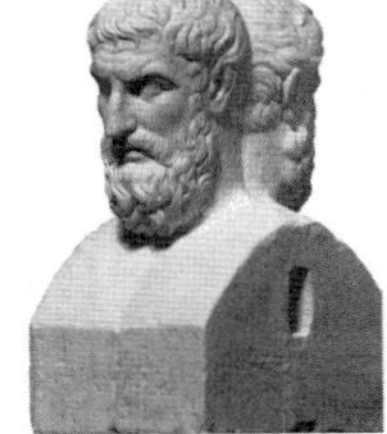

12
Ariella Azoulay has proposed the important idea of a 'civil contract' of photography in which the implicit permission to both photograph and be photographed creates a civil society in and through images that is unrelated to the commodification of, for instance, an individual photograph. See Ariella Azoulay, *The Civil Contract of Photography*, trans. Rela Mazali and Ruvik Danieli (New York, 2008), esp. pp. 85–135.

own time adequately, we cannot indulge nostalgically in Benjamin's despair at the loss of aura:

> In even the most perfect reproduction, one thing is lacking: the here and now of the work of art— its unique existence in a particular place. It is this unique existence— and nothing else—that bears the mark of the history to which the work has been subject... . The authenticity of a thing is the quintessence of all that is transmissible in it from its origin on, ranging from its physical duration to the historical testimony relating to it. Since the historical testimony is founded on the physical duration, the former, too, is jeopardized by reproduction, in which the physical duration plays no part. And what is really jeopardized when the historical testimony is affected is the authority of the object, the weight it derives from its tradition.
>
> One might focus these aspects of the artwork in the concept of the aura, and go on to say: what withers in the age of technological reproducibility of the work of art is the latter's aura.[13]

13
Walter Benjamin, *The Work of Art in the Age of Its Technological Reproducibility* (1936), 2nd version, in *Walter Benjamin: Selected Writings, Volume 3: 1935–1938*, trans. Edmund Jephcott, Howard Eiland, et al., ed. Howard Eiland and Michael W. Jennings (repr. Cambridge, 2002), pp. 103 and 104.

According to Benjamin, aura results from site-specificity. It is because the work of art belongs to a 'time and space' that it can possess the authority of a witness. Reproduction jeopardizes 'the historical testimony' and the 'authority of the object'. It eliminates distance in time and space by making the image nomadic. Aura is closely associated with image fundamentalism. But as Benjamin was well aware, one of the primary aesthetic and political struggles of modernity has been the dislocation of images from any particular site and their insertion into networks where they are characterized by motion, either potential or actual, and where they can change format—that is, experience cascading chains of relocation and remediation. Images are no longer, and probably can never again be, site-specific, in the way Benjamin understood them to be, which means that, instead of witnessing history, they constitute its very currency. This is why the restitution debates I have discussed belong to our historical moment: they represent a fundamentalist effort to restore aura at a juncture when the potential of image circulation and the population explosion of images are irreversible. They are claims of ownership of and rights to image wealth, often on the part of nations in the global South. Among the most insidious aspects of Benjamin's influence are the enduring assumptions that mechanical reproduction constitutes an absolute loss and, consequently, that commodification, which is premised on large-scale mechanical reproduction, is the worst possible fate for any cultural content (even though it is the fate of all cultural content to varying degrees). There are gains as well as losses in the shift from singular artworks to populations of images that must be acknowledged before any attempt is made to comprehend contemporary art. In their important book, *Ethnicity, Inc.*, John L. and Jean Comaroff theorize what they call the ethno-commodity, which packages life-ways or 'ethnic' heritage into an image and/or product to be sold, sometimes as the only product a community may have to trade. Such commodification of identity is one of the primary crimes mechanical reproduction is accused of, involving, as Benjamin asserts, the loss of authority, history, and authenticity. But the Comaroffs come to a dramatically different conclusion:

> [T]he ethno-commodity is a very strange thing indeed. Flying in the face of many conventional assumptions about price and value, its very appeal lies in the fact that it seems to resist ordinary economic ratio-nality. In part, this is because the quality of difference it vends may be reproduced and traded without appearing to lose its original value.

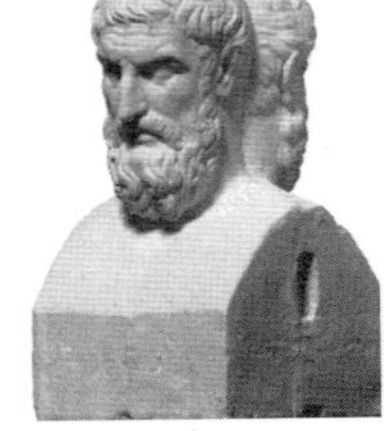

Why? Because its 'raw material' is not depleted by mass circulation. To the contrary, mass circulation reaffirms ethnicity— in general and in all its particularity—and, with it, the status of the embodied ethnic subject as a source of means of identity. Greater supply, in other words, entails greater demand.[14]

14
John L. and Jean Comaroff, *Ethnicity, Inc.* (Chicago, 2009), p. 20.

One could say, following the Comaroffs and contra Benjamin, that it is saturation through mass circulation—the status of being everywhere at once rather than belonging to a single place—that now produces value for and through images (and not only in 'ethno-commodities'). Instead of a radiating nimbus of authenticity and authority underwritten by site-specificity, we have the value of saturation, of being everywhere at once. Instead of aura, there is buzz. Like a swarm of bees, a swarm of images makes a buzz, and like a new idea or trend, once an image (whether attached to a product, a policy, a person, or a work of art) achieves saturation, it has a 'buzz' (diagram 2). The buzz arises, not from the agency of a single object or event, but from the emergent behaviours of populations of actors (both organic and inorganic) when their discrete movements are sufficiently in phase to produce coordinated action—when bees, for example, organize themselves into a swarm. Such events are not planned or directed by a single focused intelligence. They are 'distributed' over several small acts that, taken individually, may have no intention, or consciousness of a bigger picture.[15] Buzz indicates a moment of becoming—a threshold at which coherence emerges. Emergent and distributive forms are now recognized across a wide variety of fields:

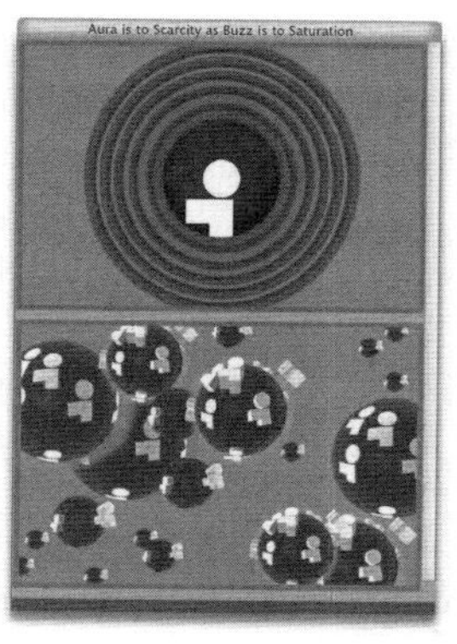

Diagram 2
Designed by Geoff Kaplan.

15
My arguments are indebted to Bruno Latour's elaboration of actor-network theory. For an introduction to this school of thought, see Bruno Latour, *Reassembling the Social: An Introduction to Actor-Network Theory* (Oxford, 2005).

* In science: Diagnosing emergent behaviours or patterns, especially with regard to chaos theory, is among the most promising and popularly evocative scientific pursuits of this century.

* In political theory: Since the publication of Michael

Hardt's and Antonio Negri's influential book Empire in 2000, the concept of the multitude constituted from extranational global movements of people—of migrants or refugees—has been linked to a special form of political agency whose demands are made, not of a particular state, but of the entire world. The authors' concepts are of a piece with the importance of non-governmental organizations and multinational corporations that produce emergent transnational communities, some devoted to philanthropy and others to pure profit.[16]

16
See Michael Hardt and Antonio Negri, *Empire* (Cambridge, 2000).

* In distributed computing and information science: The Internet would be impossible without the distribution of functional computing across networked clusters of computers situated in far-flung sites across the world. And, like all distributed networks, this one displays a robustness that derives from redundancy: you cannot disable the entire system by disabling individual nodes, since there are many others available to take over their functions.

* In popular culture: Images of people and events multiply in magnitudes that cannot be planned or anticipated. Once there is a quantitative flashpoint, fads, trends, and celebrities generate news automatically: they are capable of autonomously multiplying their images.

* In the art world: Since the 1960s, artists have pursued strategies of image saturation appropriate to populations of images, rather than inventing single works. Andy Warhol was the pioneer: he used photo silkscreen printing processes to overproduce paintings in his New York studio, the Factory. He mastered media circuits that had been outside the art world, such as film, music, advertising, and performance. And he carefully cultivated his own personal

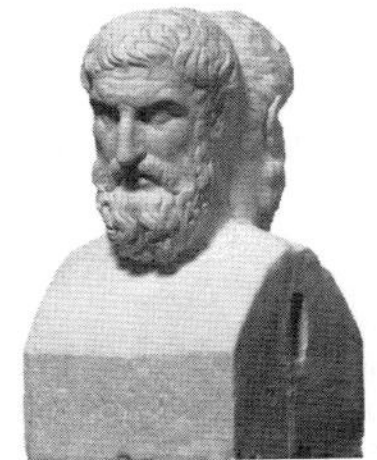

celebrity. As he put it himself, he was a 'business artist' whose work encompassed a configuration of 'product lines' rather than a succession of individual objects.[17] The emergent image is a dynamic form that arises from circulation. As such, it is located on a spectrum between the absolute stasis of native site-specificity on the one hand, and the absolute freedom of neoliberal markets on the other. Its specific location on this spectrum—its particular ratio of non-transferable native content to commercial mobility—represents its velocity as a cultural product. Take, for example, the first Chinese artists to gain prominence in the West—those associated with so-called Cynical Reason and Political Pop, such as Wang Guangyi (fig. 5). His works, which often take twentieth-century Chinese political icons as their motifs, have the perfect formula for success in a global art world: they carry a quantum of native 'Chineseness', but their mobilization of familiar Western art styles makes it possible for them to communicate this unfamiliar and even 'exotic' content to a broad range of audiences who have little knowledge of China. This is what the contemporary global artwork must be: an emissary whose power arises from cultural translation rather than from avant-garde innovation, a form of international currency that can cross borders effortlessly.

Instead of continuing to accumulate more and more artworks in the basements of museums that proliferate across the developed world, we could, without falling into monetization, take image diplomacy seriously and attempt to imagine how art can function as a currency. This would involve making cultural politics a serious dimension of foreign policy, as the rightly maligned but highly effective United States Information Agency did in the middle of the twentieth century.[18] Or it might involve regarding images as the global resources they actually are, and working towards global image justice. That would include redistributing image wealth between the global North

17
Warhol writes, 'Business art is the step that comes after Art. I started as a commercial artist, and I want to finish as a business artist, After I did the thing called "art" or whatever it's called, I went into business art. I wanted to be an Art Businessman or a Business Artist. Being good in business is the most fascinating kind of art.' Andy Warhol, *The Philosophy of Andy Warhol (From A to B and Back Again)* (San Diego, 1975), p. 92. See also Isabelle Graw, *High Price: Art between the Market and Celebrity Culture*, trans. Nicholas Grindell (Berlin, 2009).

18
For an exemplary account of the aggressive efforts of the United States to exploit the diplomatic potential of art, see Serge Guilbaut, *How New York Stole the Idea of Modern Art: Abstract Expressionism, Freedom, and the Cold War*, trans. Arthur Goldhammer (Chicago, 1983).

and South. This is indeed the sort of wise suggestion made by art historian Irene Winter in her trenchant review of James Cuno's book, *Who Owns Antiquity?* Winter points out that Cuno's faith in the Encyclopedic Art Museum as a model of enlightened multiculturalism conveniently ignores inequalities between the developed and the developing worlds. It is worth quoting one of her examples at length:

> I speak here of the mounting by Stella Kramrisch of the Manifestations of Shiva exhibition at the Philadelphia Museum of Art in the 1980s. The government of India, under the Ministry of Education and Culture, made every possible resource of staff and materials available to Philadelphia to ensure that the finest works of sculpture and painting [would] be included in the exhibition. It was agreed that the Philadelphia Museum of Art would then make 'comparable loans' available from its own collection. What the Philadelphia Museum actually offered was to loan back to India representative works of Indian art in its collection. The National Museum in New Delhi, however, already had a rather extensive collection of Indian art; what it desired was European paintings of high quality, particularly Impressionist works, that would provide a stimulating and inspiring experience for an Indian public … . The then director of the Philadelphia Museum … deemed such an exchange out of the question. So much for the third world's opportunity to exhibit the global artistic heritage.[19]

What if the United States State Department spent more time thinking about cultural diplomacy and less about making war? What if some of its budget and the budgets of European foreign ministries (as opposed to those of often marginalized ministries of culture)

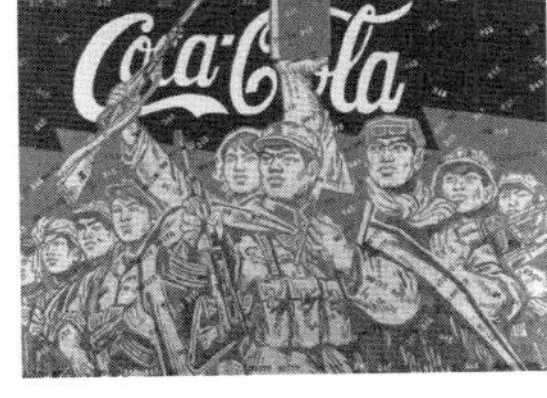

Figure 5
Wang Guangyi, *Coca Cola*, 2004, from *Great Criticism Series*. Oil on canvas, 78.7 × 118.1 in. (200 × 300 cm).

19
Irene J. Winter, 'James Cuno: Who Owns Antiquity?: Museums and the Battle over Our Ancient Heritage', *Art Bulletin* 91, no. 4 (December 2009), p. 523.

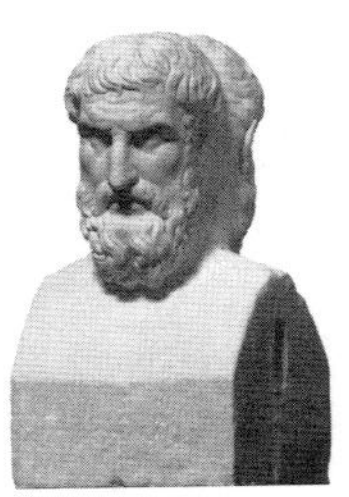

IMAGE EXPLOSION

made grants to modernize cultural infrastructure in the global South so that directors of institutions such as the Philadelphia Museum of Art could never cite inadequate facilities as an excuse for denying cultural exchange. (The Greek government built its new Acropolis Museum in Athens precisely to take away the possibility of such excuses). And why is the vast majority of the cultural wealth in the industrialized world sitting in storage? Indeed, the proliferation of museums worldwide, and the policies of stockpiling pursued by the richest of them, complicate the distinction I have made here between neoliberal and fundamentalist modes of circulation. I have argued that the former privileges the unlimited mobility of works of art, while the latter is rooted in the conviction that works of art should remain in their place of origin. But the neoliberal position has its own form of conservatism that verges on fundamentalism: the collection and conservation of works of art in museums, which replace the individual artwork's 'natural habitat' by establishing cosmopolitan cultural centres—or central banks—to house them. This is the type of capital accumulation that museums speculate on by organizing national and international travelling exhibitions, globalizing their collections (as in the satellites of the Guggenheim Museum, the Louvre, and the Hermitage), and deriving significant revenues from their holdings by reproducing them in souvenirs, publications, and authorized reproductions in museum stores. This is a currency of art that, as in hedge funds in the metropolitan West, has been hoarded and leveraged to benefit the few. We should think as democratically as we can about image circulation, begin to consider what a redistribution of image wealth might look like, and use the currency of art for purposes other than financial gain.

This is a slightly modified version of an essay that first appeared in my book *After Art* (Princeton, 2013), pp. 1–23. Courtesy of Princeton University Press.

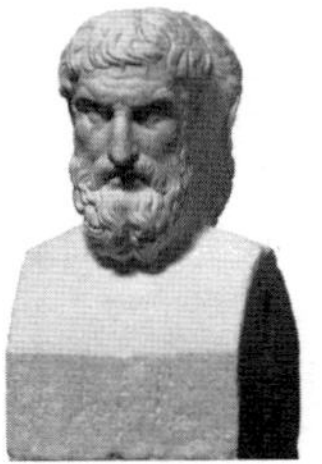

IMAGE EXPLOSION

AGAINST THE NOVELTY OF NEW MEDIA
MEDIA
The Resuscitation of the Authentic

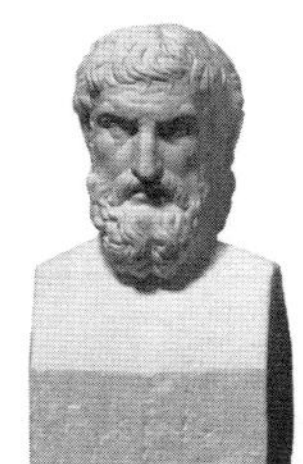

Erika Balsom

'As words that are sacred without sacred content, as frozen emanations, the terms of the jargon of authenticity are products of the disintegration of the aura.'
—Theodor Adorno[1]

At dOCUMENTA (13) in 2012, Artistic Director Carolyn Christov-Bakargiev made much of the notion that her exhibition lacked any unifying theme. And yet, amongst the many threads running throughout, one was particularly prominent: an interest in what one critic called 'the emplaced condition of things'.[2] In the rotunda of the Fridericianum—dubbed the 'brain' of the exhibition—a number of objects exemplified this concern: four-thousand-year-old Bactrian princess figurines from Central Asia, artefacts from the National Museum in Beirut that had been damaged during the Lebanese Civil War, and the painting Mohammad Yusuf Asefi saved from destruction at the hands of the Taliban by painting over any human figures. These are objects inscribed by time, as far away from free-floating signifiers as one can get. To put it in Benjamin's terms: they privilege cult value over exhibition value.[3] They are singular objects, inextricable from their respective material histories, absolutely incompatible with the compress-and-copy life of a JPEG. Against both the textualist model of culture that was such a prominent component of postmodernism, and the frenzied circulation proper to globalization in the digital age, here, as throughout much of dOCUMENTA (13), one finds a return to the referent, to the eminently *authentic*.[4]

The deployment of authenticity in dOCUMENTA (13) is notable in part because it participated in the rehabilitation of a notion that had previously been rather out of fashion, if not since Adorno allied its jargon with fascism, then certainly after the poststructuralist critique of essence and origin. The rhetoric of authenticity partakes of notions

1

Theodor Adorno, *The Jargon of Authenticity*, trans. Knut Tarnowski and Frederic Will (Evanston, 1973), pp. 9–10.

2

Steven Henry Madoff, 'Why Curator Carolyn Christov-Bakargiev's Documenta May Be the Most Important Exhibition of the 21st Century', *Blouin Artinfo*, published 5 July 2012, www.blouinartinfo.com/news/story/811949/why-curator-carolyn-christov-bakargievs-documenta-may-be-the-most-important-exhibition-of-the-21st-century (accessed 25 July 2013).

3

See Walter Benjamin, 'The Work of Art in the Age of Its Technological Reproducibility (Second Version)', trans. Edmund Jephcott and Harry Zohn, in *Selected Writings, Volume 3: 1935–1938*, ed. Howard Eiland and Michael W. Jennings (Cambridge, 2002), p. 105.

of pure beginnings and implicitly denigrates what comes later, which is marked as corrupting or contaminating. In this regard, the relative lack of engagement with digital culture in dOCUMENTA (13) is striking. For Adorno, discourses of authenticity offered a rearticulation of the ideology of National Socialism by other means; for the poststructuralists, they were guilty of a metaphysical investment in presence and identity valorized at the expense of recognizing difference. For all of these reasons, authenticity was left behind in favour of hybridity, reproducibility, and purposeful unoriginality.

Today, however, authenticity is undeniably back. In its concern with authentic objects, dOCUMENTA (13) is far from alone. Massimiliano Gioni's 'The Encyclopedic Palace', the headline exhibition at the 2013 Venice Biennale, privileged madness, the unconscious and outsiders situated far from the commodification of the art system, thus implicitly contesting the professionalization of the artist as a betrayal of that figure's exemplary authenticity.[5] Whether in Rudolf Steiner's blackboards, Shinichi Sawada's spiked figurines or Eva Kotátková's collaboration with psychiatric patients, throughout the exhibition one found repeated gestures towards forms of artistic production supposedly motivated by deep and pure urges, rather than by money, fame, or a linear narrative of art-historical intervention. As the placement of Camille Henrot's video *Grosse Fatigue* (2013) near the entrance of the Arsenale made clear, Gioni's exhibition was very much about (among other things) the notion that the Internet constitutes but the latest iteration of a long-standing desire to create totalizing systems of knowledge. And yet, though the Internet provided a framework through which one might view 'The Encyclopedic Palace', one could equally say that the exhibition largely rejected the new media landscape as shallow and decorporealized.

4

Hal Foster saw this turn already in art of the early 1990s. He writes, 'From a conventionalist regime in which nothing is real and the subject is superficial, much contemporary art presents reality in the form of trauma and the subject in the social depth of its own identity. After the apotheosis of the signifier and the symbolic, then, we are witness to a *turn to the real* on the one hand and a *turn to the referent* on the other.' See Hal Foster, *The Return of the Real: The Avant-Garde at the End of the Century* (Cambridge, MA, 1996), p. 124. Emphasis in text.

5

As Luc Boltanski and Eve Chiapello have noted, the life of the nineteenth-century artist was considered to be a particular wellspring of authenticity because 'it was not compartmentalized but succeeded in unifying all the facets of the same existence, and gearing it towards the completion of an oeuvre and the uniqueness of its creator'. Luc Boltanski and Eve Chiapello, *The New Spirit of Capitalism*, trans. Gregory Elliott (London, 2005), p. 472, note 5.

The three spiritual fathers governing the exhibition—Jung, Steiner, and Breton—embrace a depth-model of the subject closely tied to the notion of authenticity as a moral imperative, one that is exceedingly far from both the depersonalized intensities of the Deleuzian subject and the anti-anthropocentrism of the speculative realists.

Beyond exhibitions such as dOCUMENTA (13) and 'The Encyclopedic Palace', outmoded technologies appear regularly in galleries around the world, while craft has made a palpable return. 16-mm film projection stages a contestation of the ubiquity and novelty of the digital image, with figures such as Luther Price and Paolo Cherchi Usai privileging the materiality of the medium and claiming it as a damaged, living body subject to entropic decay. The artist Tino Sehgal's refusal to document his own work further rehearses the attachment to singularity and presence that characterizes much of contemporary performance. However, authenticity is not simply a feature of today's art: it is equally prominent in contemporary marketing strategies, particularly as they are deployed in the domains of food and travel. The names of purveyors of artisanal greens abound on menus, while 'untouched' travel destinations—trekking in Bhutan, for example—offer unprecedented appeal.

What all of these examples share is an allergy to the mass (re)production of images, experiences, subjects, and objects. These examples position themselves against ubiquity and against the exchange principle. They elevate the anachronism of the authentic above a present seen as brimming with the unreal, the false, the amnesic, and the prepackaged. What is at stake in such a resuscitation of authenticity? Can it be anything other than reactionary? How might this new fetish for the authentic function as a significant, if sometimes spurious, post-digital cultural formation? Tracing the evolution of the concept of authenticity from its roots in the Romantic imaginary through its mobilization in nineteenth-century critiques of modernity and into the present might provide a way of beginning to answer these questions.

6

Edward Young, *Conjectures on Original Composition* (London, 1759), p. 42.

In his 1759 text 'Conjectures on Original Composition', Edward Young asks: 'Born Originals, how comes it to pass that we die *Copies*?'[6] Young's question is rooted in a Romantic conviction, primarily associated with the thought of Jean-Jacques Rousseau, that society is destructive of the authenticity and goodness of humankind. In the nineteenth century, such ideas found increased currency as new processes of urbanization and technologization forever altered the subject's relationship to nature, time, work, and leisure. Industrial modernity proceeded as a rationalization of all aspects of life driven by a capitalist economy, prompting some to see it not as progress but rather as experiential impoverishment. As an emblem of this collapse of difference, the copy is particularly denigrated. Very much in line with Young's rhetoric, mid-nineteenth-century works of literature such as Charles Dickens's *A Christmas Carol* (1843) and Herman Melville's *Bartelby, The Scrivener: A Story of Wall Street* (1853) communicated the extinguishing of the soul experienced by their main protagonists by casting them in the profession of manual copyist.[7] It is worth noting that the conceptualization of copying by hand found in these texts represents a significant shift from an earlier understanding of the activity, namely its practice by monks, whereby it figured as an erudite occupation integral to the transmission of knowledge. Now, copying becomes mere drudgery, a synecdoche used to point to how the interconnectedness and fidelity to tradition that had characterized pre-modern society now found itself destroyed in the rise of the modern *Gesellschaft*, in which atomization and self-interest prevailed. Copying, long a neutral activity, was degraded and devalued because of its close ties to mechanization and standardization, while objects that evaded the regime of duplicated sameness were exalted as more precious, more human.

7

For an extended discussion of the figure of the copyist in nineteenth-century fiction and an inventory of its appearances, see Rima Shore, 'Scrivener Fiction: The Copyist and His Craft in Nineteenth-Century Fiction', unpublished PhD dissertation, Columbia University, 1980.

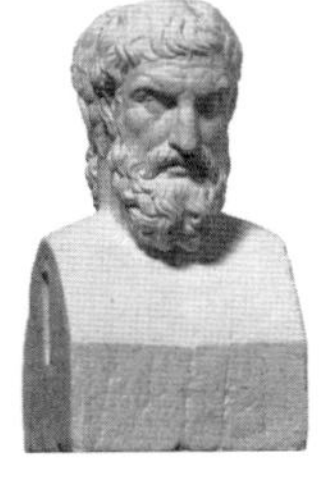

AGAINST THE NOVELTY OF NEW MEDIA

Young's assertion that we are born originals articulates a conviction that we begin life as essentially true to ourselves before experiencing a progressive estrangement from this state that takes the form of a false outer self concerned with being-for-others—something Sartre would much later term 'bad faith'. Rather than a yearning for originality, a term that became attached to the artistic vanguard's penchant for radical novelty, this sentiment is better understood as the desire for authenticity. The authentic is, in other words, first and foremost a subjective ideal invested with a heavy moral weight. It is a polemical concept that seeks to revive a fullness of meaning and an unalienated state of being at a time when increased secularization and industrialization prompted a crisis of absolutes. In the absence of the transcendent and the eternal, the subject turns inward to find their 'true' self, different from that of all others. Likewise, in Venice, the prominent display of pages from Jung's *Red Book* (1914–1930) signalled the importance the exhibition accorded to the notion of turning inward and probing the deep recesses of the psyche. The commercial art world, it was implicitly suggested, is an exemplary realm of bad faith in which artists act according to how they believe that world wishes them to. 'The Encyclopedic Palace' countered this prevailing inauthenticity by showcasing individuals who demonstrated persistent investments in absoluteness and spirituality, even if this meant including a relatively small number of contemporary practitioners in a venue tasked with displaying the best of today's art.

Though authenticity is a subjective ideal, it stems from the world of objects—specifically, from the museum—and quickly returns there, as technology, industry, and the products of mass culture become identified with an inauthenticity that threatens the individuality of the individual. With an etymology meaning 'self made', authenticity is by definition anti-technological and elevates the human above the new machines. As Lionel Trilling writes in his landmark 1972 study, *Sincerity and Authenticity*:

The anxiety about the machine is a commonplace in nineteenth-century moral and cultural thought… It was the mechanical principle, quite as much as the acquisitive principle—the two are of course intimately connected—which was felt to be the enemy of being, the source of inauthenticity. The machine, said Ruskin, could only make inauthentic things, dead things; and the dead things communicated their deadness to those who used them.[8]

8
Lionel Trilling, *Sincerity and Authenticity* (Cambridge, 1972), pp. 126–127.

The authentic is, then, presumed to be outside the regime of equivalence that drives commodity exchange, and also outside the sphere of reproducibility. It is thus closely allied with nature, art, craft, and earlier forms of existence. One encounters a partitioning of the world wherein what is authentic is opposed to what is new. Older modes of image-making and traditional forms of experience are valorized because they are seen to offer a reassuring escape from the instability and uncertainty of the rapidly changing present. It is in this context that one can begin understanding the fetish for craft and the outmoded that has prevailed in recent artistic production: it is against the supposed 'deadness' of the digital copy that the dOCUMENTA (13) 'brain' offered ceramics by Julia Isidrez and Juana Marta Rodas. Within the authenticity paradigm, the relationship between subject and object is conceived as one of mimetic contagion: just as Ruskin believed 'dead things communicated their deadness to those who used them', so might the authentic endow those who encounter it with an increased moral standing through a kind of sympathetic magic.

Concerns with authenticity were central to lapsarian critiques of modernity and technology in the late nineteenth and early twentieth centuries, whether in Max Weber's thesis that modernity constitutes the disenchantment of the world or Walter

Benjamin's notion of the decay of aura. In the nineteenth century, clock time, the cinema, and the assembly line were all inauthentic novelties threatening traditional, authentic forms of existence and image production. Today, supposedly untrustworthy digital images and seemingly depersonalized electronic-communications technologies are taking over this role. We are undergoing a moment that is, in a way, parallel to that in the nineteenth century: once again, there has been a qualitative shift in the reproducibility of images and sounds, and a major acceleration in the temporality of obsolescence. These technological changes occurred in conjunction with economic deregulation, the restructuring of labour, and the remapping of global flows of people, capital, and information. In short, they occurred as a part of a transformation of experience just as immense and wide-ranging as that which occurred in the nineteenth century. Once again, a desire for authenticity has emerged as a reaction to shifts with new-media technologies at their core. Scour the discourses of the digital pessimists—from Baudrillard to Virilio and others—and echoes of the nineteenth century will ring in one's ears. Against the promiscuous circulation of proliferating copies, the singular event of performance and the uniqueness of the handmade object both emerge as sites of intense cathexis. Even photochemical film—once the exemplary inauthentic image—can now be recuperated as authentic, as the images of electronic reproduction have arrived to occupy the denigrated position it once held.

For Benjamin, the status of authenticity was vexed. It was valued as a site of resistance to the dehumanization and disenchantment of capitalist exchange, but deplored for its class character. Access to the authentic, after all, tends to be fairly exclusive. Understood in this second sense, the desire for authenticity is no escape from commodity fetishism but its apotheosis: it is a way of dissimulating a relationship to economic privilege by cloaking a yearning for the rare and expensive in spiritual, Romantic terms. Moreover, Adorno fully recognized that, despite authenticity's claims to origins and intrinsic value, it is always retroactively constructed and resides fully within the paradigm of commodity exchange:

> Only when countless standardized commodities project, for the sake of profit, the illusion of being unique, does the idea take shape, as their antithesis yet in keeping with the same criteria, that the non-reproducible is truly genuine.[9]

9

Theodor Adorno, *Minima Moralia: Reflections on a Damaged Life*, trans. E.F.N. Jephcott (London, 2005), p. 155.

This notion of a false projection of uniqueness stemming from a ground of sameness is particularly apposite in the era of iEverything. If Fordist capitalism succeeded in producing seductive commodities that delivered the ever-same as the ever-new, the contemporary moment witnesses the continuance of this regime, supplemented by a digital marketplace promising the seemingly infinite variety of the long tail and the fantasy of totally individualized consumption. When everything appears to be available at the click of a mouse, even more strongly does the idea take shape that 'the non-reproducible is truly genuine' and even more strongly felt is the lure of the authentic.

In their 2007 book, *Authenticity: What Consumers Really Want*, business management writers James H. Gilmore and B. Joseph Pine seize on this desire for the authentic as a new customer sensibility on which entrepreneurs might capitalize. They write:

> In a world increasingly filled with deliberately and sensationally staged experiences—in an increasingly *unreal* world—customers choose to buy or not buy based on how *real* they perceive an offering to be. Business today, therefore, is all about being real. Original. Genuine. Sincere. *Authentic.*[10]

10

James H. Gilmore and B. Joseph Pine II, *Authenticity: What Consumers Really Want* (Cambridge, MA, 2007), p. 1. Emphasis in text.

This idea accords marketing strategies

the same role that has historically been accorded to art: to provide an alternative to what is. Except here, rather than any true challenge to affirmative culture, the goal is to sell products through an operation that dissimulates its relationship to commodity exchange by superficially adopting the guise of precisely that which is supposed to reside outside of it, the authentic. In a world of 'technological intrusion', Pine and Gilmore argue, businesses can add value by 'rendering authenticity'.[11] Guidelines for doing so include an absolute prohibition on declarations of authenticity ('It's easier to *be* authentic if you don't *say* you're authentic') and an imperative to 'humanize' all interactions customers have with technology.

Gilmore and Pine became known within the art world when their book, *The Experience Economy: Work is a Theatre and Every Business a Stage*, was discussed by critics interested in understanding how the practices grouped under the heading of relational aesthetics might dovetail with broader transformations of capital.[12] Taking Walt Disney as a foundational example—one that notably also features prominently in Baudrillard's *Simulations*, albeit in a negative capacity—the strategies elaborated in *The Experience Economy* were meant to instruct businesses on how to offer something unusual, something that would make customers feel as if it has been crafted just for them, such as when the cashier puts their name on a cup at Starbucks. If there is a correlation between the marketing strategies described in *The Experience Economy* and a privileging of relationality in the art of the 1990s, is it now possible to say that the focus on authenticity as a consumer sensibility is also paralleled by particular kinds of artistic and curatorial practices that privilege authenticity? And if so, does this isomorphism with market logic neutralize whatever criticality those practices might purport to possess?

A crucial difference between those practices correlated with the 'experience economy' and those aligned with the desire for authenticity is that the former made no claims

11
Ibid., p. 14.

12
See Claire Bishop, 'Antagonism and Relational Aesthetics', *October* 110 (Fall 2004), pp. 51–79.

of residence outside the dominant cultural logic. Indeed, though Nicolas Bourriaud made emancipatory claims on behalf of particular artists, in many cases a closer examination of their work reveals a cannily ambivalent relationship to the transformations of capital and labour that occurred in the 1990s.[13] Authenticity, by contrast, derives its force from posing as an alternative to, rather than an engagement with, the status quo. It seeks to remedy a supposed lack; it is a fundamentally conservative withdrawal from the present. For some, this is enough to mark it as reactionary and disqualify it as a viable strategy. Steven Shaviro, for example, has opposed so-called 'slow cinema' on these grounds. Filmmakers such as Apichatpong Weerasethakul, Béla Tarr, and Tsai Ming-liang pursue protracted narrativity and extremely long takes, creating a cinema that prizes durational experience as a way of escaping a contemporary everyday that seems to accelerate uncontrollably. In Shaviro's view, rather than a direct engagement with the contradictions of contemporary experience, such filmmaking constitutes 'an evasive cop-out', 'a profound failure of the imagination', and a 'retreat into fantasies of the good old days'.[14] One might say the same thing of the deployment of authenticity in contemporary art, setting it against the work of artists who straightforwardly confront the vicissitudes of digital existence. But while such a criticism might apply to a young artist who decides to cultivate a precious ceramics practice, can the objects included in the dOCUMENTA (13) 'brain' be dismissed so easily?

Though the various deployments of authenticity may be united in their shared status as rearguard responses to anxieties provoked by the ubiquity and perceived sameness of digital culture, it is necessary to mark out some distinctions between and among them. When the end of a tourism advertisement for the remote Canadian province

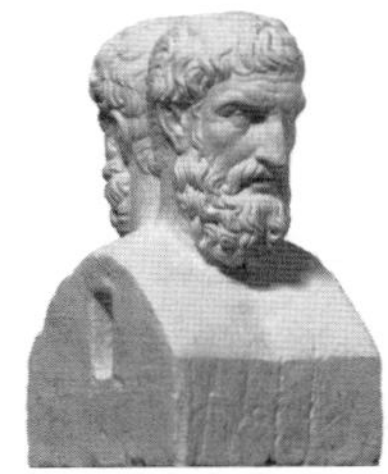

13
Compare, for example, Bourriaud's gloss of Pierre Huyghe with the more rigorous and attentive assessment of the artist undertaken by Tom McDonough in 'No Ghost', *October* 110 (Fall 2004), pp. 107–130.

14
Shaviro looks to films such as *Southland Tales* (2006) and *Gamer* (2009) as successful attempts at grappling with the contradictions of contemporary existence. Steven Shaviro, 'Slow Cinema vs. Fast Films', published 12 March 2010, www.shaviro.com/Blog/?p=891 (accessed 29 July 2013).

     AGAINST THE NOVELTY OF NEW MEDIA

of Newfoundland asks the viewer to 'Call Joan' for more information, this falsely personal touch is nothing other than the staging of a spurious pseudo-authenticity. Of course 'Joan' won't be on the other end of the line, but as the authentic is always closely allied with the human and against the machine, the idea of calling 'Joan' is much more enticing and consonant with the image of the province the campaign seeks to project than calling an automated telephone menu would be. But in an encounter with the damaged artefacts from the National Museum in Beirut at dOCUMENTA (13), the force of time and the absolute singularity of the objects are palpable. These mangled pieces of metal and glass challenge the notion that the value of the art object is a matter of aesthetics alone, and instead suggest the extent to which social and political relations may be embedded in the materiality of things. These are not objects isolated from the passage of time but rather poignant testimonies of violence and trauma. They are obstinate reminders of the contingent circumstances by which some things endure while others perish.

Though Adorno articulated a scathing critique of the place of authenticity in an administered world, he did nonetheless hold on to the validity of an honorific use of the word, one that locates the authentic in what is vulnerable and transient rather than pure and fixed. As he writes: 'Scars of damage and disruption are the modern's seal of authenticity; by their means, art desperately negates the closed confines of the ever-same...'[15] Though the objects in the 'brain' invoke the rhetoric of singularity and authenticity, they recognize the arrogance and artificiality of an easy return to origins, and instead locate the authentic in those objects that index, rather than deny, the frailty and difficulty of being in the world. In doing so, they repudiate any retreat into a reified and glorified past, while also proposing a different relationship to history than is most often found in contemporary manifestations of technocapitalism. Unlike the return to a depth model of

15
Theodor Adorno, *Aesthetic Theory*, trans. Robert Hullot-Kentor (London, 2004), p. 29.

the subject, such a consideration of the life of objects may be understood as avoiding some of the pitfalls of the old authenticity discourses while maintaining the ability to mobilize the anachronism of the authentic as a challenge to our present.

The resuscitation of the authentic is, then, a persistent reminder that there is both a danger and a value in the rejection of things as they are. What's more, the resuscitation offers the striking proposal that understanding what counts as 'art after the Internet' might necessitate expanding one's purview far beyond artworks produced through digital means if one is to truly take account of the breadth of engagements with digital culture found in contemporary practice—be they reactionary or not.

This is a slightly modified version of an essay that first appeared in *You Are Here: Art After the Internet*, Omar Kholeif (ed.) (Manchester/London, 2013), pp. 66–77. Courtesy of Cornerhouse, Manchester and Space, London.

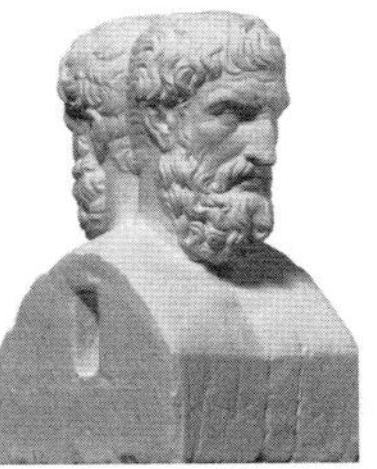

     AGAINST THE NOVELTY OF NEW MEDIA

DIGITAL PROVENANCE AND THE WORK OF ART AS DERIVATIVE

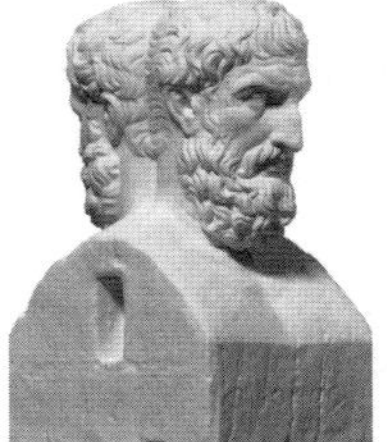

McKenzie Wark

1

Hito Steyerl, 'If You Don't
Have Bread, Eat Art!:
Contemporary Art and
Derivative Fascisms', *e-flux
Journal* #76 (October
2016).

Unlike Hito Steyerl, I don't think art is a currency.[1] I think it's a derivative, which is not quite the same thing. A currency can store value or act as a means of exchange. A derivative does something different. It manages and hedges risk. What we need, then, is a theory of art as a derivative.

Let's start with this paradox. Art is about rarity, about things that are unique and special and cannot be duplicated. And yet the technologies of our time are all about duplication, copies, about information that is not really special at all. At first, it might appear that the traditional form of art is obsolete. If it has value, it is as something from a past way of life, before information technology took over. But actually, what appears to be happening is stranger than that. Let's look at some of the special ways in which art as rarity interacts now in novel ways with information as plenty, producing some rather striking opportunities to create value.

By way of illustration, I want to discuss some art from twenty years ago. Sometime in the mid-nineties, the artist Mel Chin was watching television. He saw the actress Heather Locklear on the screen, but what the artist saw was not

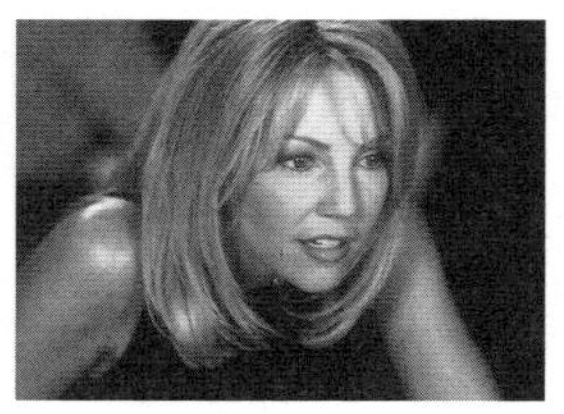

the actress, he saw the space in which she appeared: the television screen itself. What he saw there was the biggest art gallery in the world. So he contacted the set decorator for the show, whose name was Deborah Siegel. He proposed that the set should include work by artists. The artists would not be paid. They took this idea to the producers, who approved—probably because of the not-getting-paid part.

So Chin formed a group called the GALA Committee. GALA stood for Georgia and Los Angeles, and would involve artists and art students from both locations. The work was all made collaboratively. For two years, GALA worked with the scriptwriters and made art that appeared on the show, usually in the background, but sometimes thematically related to stories going on in the show and sometimes relating to things from real life. GALA made about 200 objects, the

                                          AUTHENTICITY?

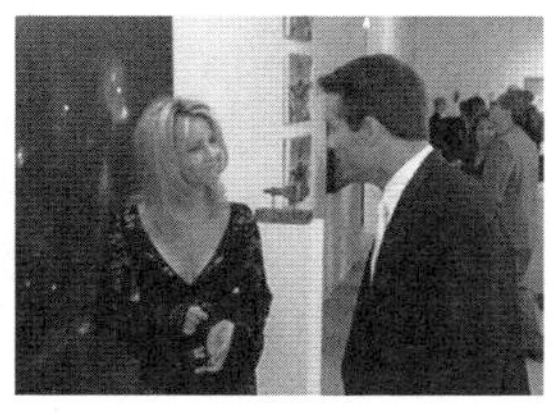

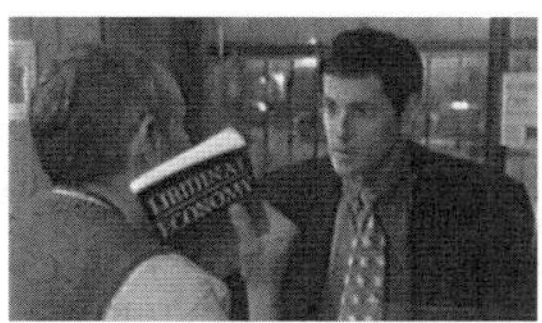

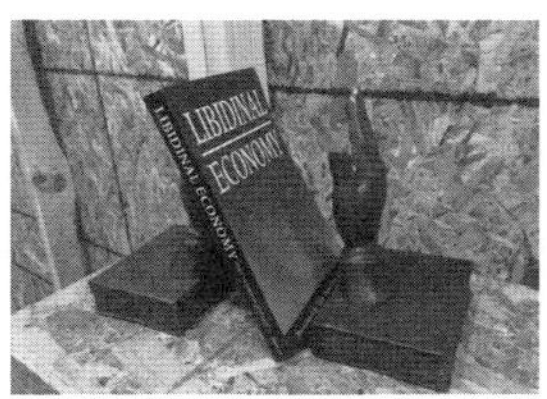

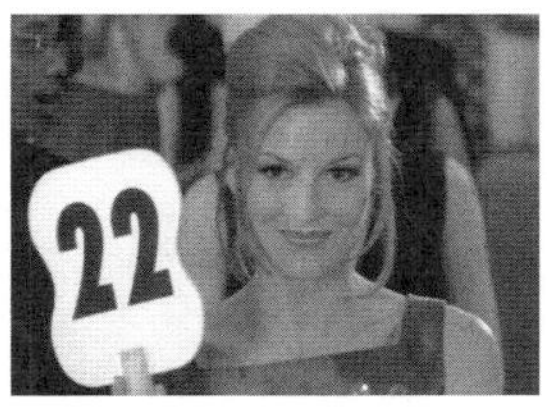

majority of which ended up on the show. The show was *Melrose Place*, one of the most iconic soap operas of its era. The GALA art was on it for two seasons, 4 and 5.

The writers eventually wrote the art into the show. One character was an artist. The Heather Locklear character, who ran an advertising agency, signed the real Los Angeles Museum of Contemporary Art (MOCA) to her made-up ad agency, and there were scenes in the show filmed at the real MOCA, showing a real exhibition of the GALA art from the show itself. The GALA art was then auctioned at Sotheby's Beverley Hills, where a real consortium of collectors from Germany bought the art. The proceeds were donated by GALA to charities.

Now: here is the detail I want to point out about all this. In the Sotheby's auction catalog, there is a list in the back that details the episodes of the show in which each work appeared. What is this list about? One word for it is provenance. What makes each piece authentic is that it appeared on a set for a television show, was videotaped on that set, and ended up in a show that was broadcast to millions of people. The show is actually still being broadcast, as *Melrose Place* is still in syndication somewhere on the planet even to this day. The provenance of the work is a really strange kind of product placement.

The New York retrospective of the GALA Committee work made me think of it as an example.[2] I think it's a nice anticipation of where we ended up in the relationship between art and information. For those who have read their Walter Benjamin, it is an interesting wrinkle in the relation that is supposed to hold between the work of art and reproducibility.[3] In Benjamin, reproducibility is supposed to undermine the aura of the work, its ritual seclusion, and above all its *provenance*, that is, its standing as a unique piece of private property. While it is conventional to treat aura as the key to how Benjamin

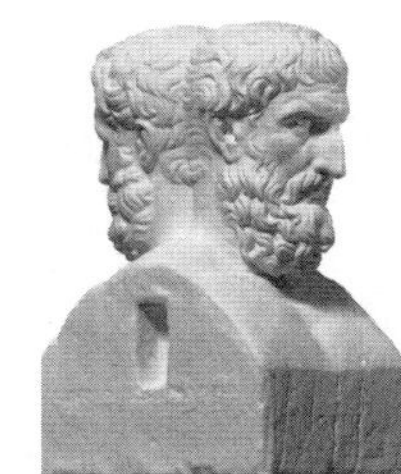

2
www.redbullstudios
newyork.com/artists/
gala-committee/.

3
Walter Benjamin, *The Work of Art in the Age of Its Technological Reproducibility, and Other Writings on Media* (Cambridge, MA, 2008).

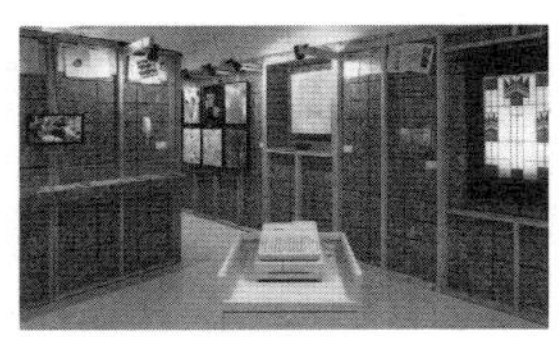

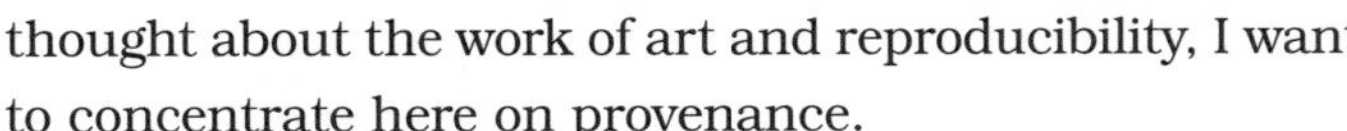

4
Hito Steyerl, *In Defense of the Poor Image, e-flux Journal* #10 (November 2009).

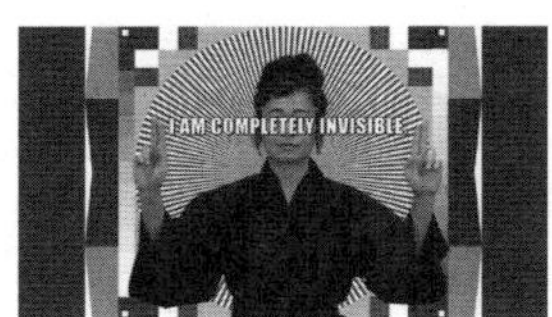

5
Jean Baudrillard, *Simulations* (Los Angeles, 2016).

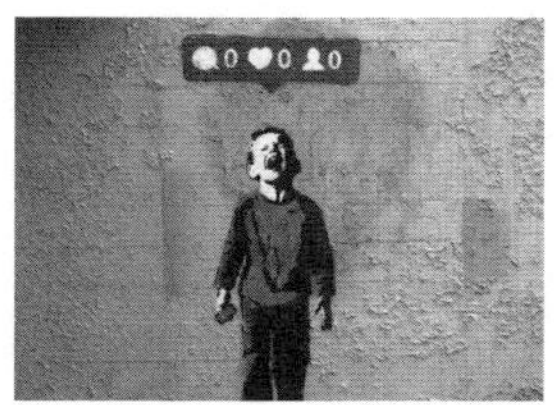

thought about the work of art and reproducibility, I want to concentrate here on provenance.

It is the reproduction of the artwork on television, electronically rather than mechanically, that, perversely enough, makes it rare. This is rather strange, given that the image of the GALA work in the TV show is what Hito Steyerl calls a poor image, a wretched image, compressed and degraded and freely available now on the internet.[4] But the GALA work itself is not thus compressed and degraded. The reproduction of the work on television in the show, and then of the show on the internet is, oddly enough, the thing that gives the GALA work nested within it its provenance. Usually, the provenance of the work has to do with the singular place of its creation and persistence. A Renaissance altar piece takes its provenance from the church of which it was an integral part for centuries. An easel-painting by a recognized master may be more portable, but it comes from the master's studio. The GALA work is different. Its provenance derives from the place of its electronic reproduction—from television. It's a kind of network or distributed provenance, perhaps.

Far from making the work of art obsolete, the reproducibility of the image can give it a new kind of value. It is not quite the case that the original and the copy become indistinguishable. But it is the case that their relationship can be reversible. The copy can precede the original. You see a reproduction of something, and that makes you want to go see the thing of which it is the copy. That's a common enough occurrence, and something Jean Baudrillard flagged some time ago.[5] But the thing to pay attention to is that the copy also creates the *provenance* of the original, not the other way around. The copy not only precedes but *authenticates* the original.

The copy can create value for the work, or in some cases for the artist rather than the work. This would be the Banksy story. The thing about Banksy that matters the most is the copies of the pieces that circulate on the

                                                  AUTHENTICITY?

Has Banksy been unmasked? Scientific study of heat maps normally used to catch criminals claims to have finally confirmed identity of mystery street artist

- Researchers used a statistical technique of geographic profiling
- Geo-profiling is more commonly used by police to catch criminals
- The scientist's results led to one prominent figure - Robin Gunningham
- Mail on Sunday named Banksy as Gunningham after an investigation

By ANTHONY JOSEPH FOR MAILONLINE
PUBLISHED: 05:58 EST, 4 March 2016 | UPDATED: 13:03 EST, 4 March 2016

815 shares · 503 View comments

A scientific study of heat maps claims to have finally unmasked the mystery of street artist Banksy.

Researchers at Queen Mary University of London used a statistical technique of geographic profiling, which is more commonly used by police to catch criminals.

6
Eli Rosenberg, 'Banksy Identified by Scientists. Maybe', *New York Times*, 7 March 2016.

7
https://vimeo. com/135392103.

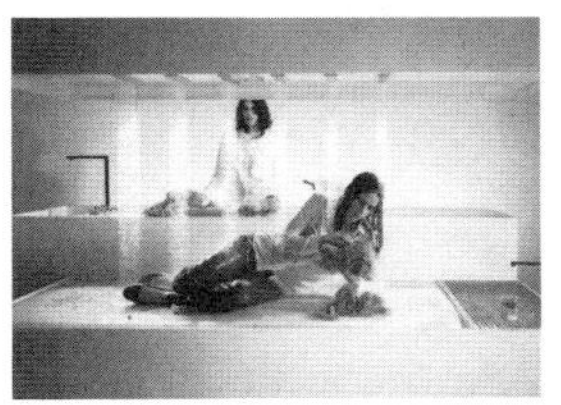

internet. That is what establishes their provenance. These appear to be works made illegally in public, but that in itself is not all that interesting or important. There's a lot of street art. It is just that this street art is authenticated by the circulation of its images. Those poor images are what creates value, in this case for a *visibly* invisible artist.

A visibly invisible artist is something of a provenance anomaly, the scene of a crime. While there has been speculation for some years now that Banksy is 'actually' a man named Robin Gunningham, the *Daily Mail* brought forensic methods from criminal investigation to bear on the question, trying to correlate known Banksy works in London with places Gunningham is known to frequent.[6] This is an example, perhaps, of counter-provenance, of layering an authentication from the world of criminal investigations over an art-world authentication.

Sometimes the preceding image that authenticates the work is not of the work even though it precedes it. As an example, I'd like to look at *The Island (Ken),* by the group that calls itself *Dis*, which was shown at the New Museum. I did a little talk-performance with this piece, and in the process of writing it I did a studio visit and talked to the artists.[7] They told me that the process that resulted in this work started with an idea about high-end kitchens and bathrooms. Googling that generated a series of advertisements based on the search terms, for companies offering such high-end appliances. So *Dis* simply chose the most high-end-seeming one and approached the company about making the pieces. Thus, in this case, the provenance of the work comes from a Google search.

This is what the Google algorithm, customizing itself for this particular computer used by *Dis*, thinks is the real thing when it comes to fancy appliances. Yet, when I searched for 'high end shower', I got slightly different

   DIGITAL PROVENANCE AND THE WORK OF ART AS DERIVATIVE

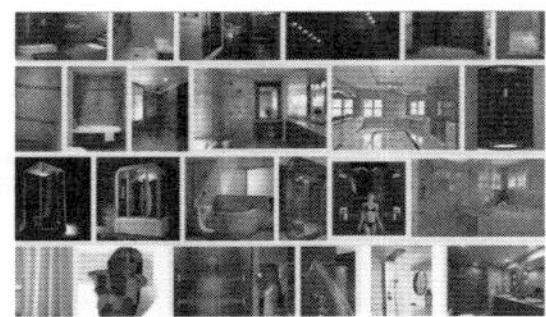

results, tailored algorithmically to me, or rather to my computer. The *signature* is in this case the algorithmically generated search, and it can be expected to differ in some way in each instance. Here we have a contrast with the GALA work, which depends on the uniformity of the broadcast model of simulation.

The artwork is now a *derivative* of its simulation. Of course, there are many different kinds of simulation, such as the jpeg of a particular work sent by a dealer to a collector as an attachment to a text message. The collector reads the text, looks at the jpeg, and makes a decision about the artwork. But actually, the artwork is a derivative. It was the jpeg that mattered, just as it is the jpeg on which the transaction depends. The collector might decide to buy or

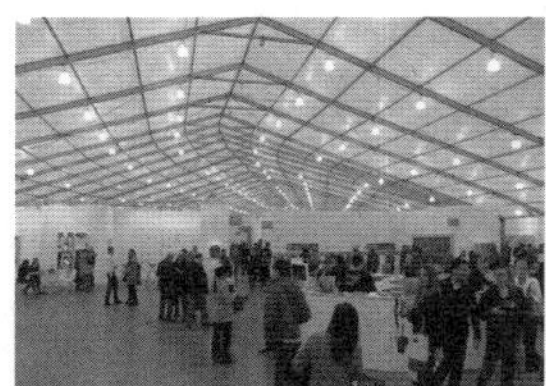

not buy the work, to reserve it, or see it later in person, and so on. As in other fields centred around financial transactions, the main thing traded here is the derivatives. The simulations are not worth much at all, or are such poor images they might as well be gifts.

It is not just individual works of art that are now derivatives of their simulations. Art itself is also such a derivative. A key to this development is the rise of art fairs and biennials. The art fairs are more directly about selling artwork derivatives of their simulated images. They are mostly about the commercial dealers who trade in the derivative contracts that are works of art themselves. But the other side of this is the biennial, whose function is to simulate contemporary art itself.

The artwork is a derivative of its simulation, or rather of its simulations. This is the way the actual, particular artwork can still work as a sort of hedge. An artwork is a risky proposition. It might, in the long run, turn out to be worth no more than any random bit of painted canvas. But if the artwork can be a *portfolio* of different kinds of simulation of itself, it is possible to manage the risk.

An artwork can be a derivative of the simulation of itself, where its image precedes it and authenticates it through its circulation and exposure. Here GALA is the example. But an artwork can also be a derivative of the simulation of its artist. And here Banksy is a slightly aberrant example, where it's the simulation of the artist's absence that created provenance. An artwork can also claim provenance from celebrity. This is one of the things going on in the commerce among the artworld, fashion, and pop music. Those mass-simulation forms think they gain something from the provenance of the artwork as a rare and singular commodity, and perhaps they do. But I think really the secret is that it is the artwork that acquires its provenance from proximity to Jay-Z or Kanye or Björk. The artwork becomes a derivative of contact with the body behind the simulation of the pop star or fashion star.

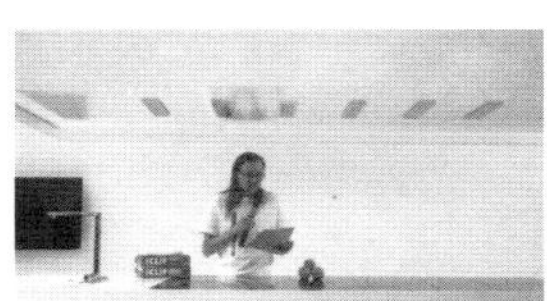

An artwork can also be a derivative of intellectual provenance. It helps if the intellectual is dead. Hence Thomas Hirschhorn's *Gramsci Monument*, which derives its provenance from a famous dead communist thinker. If one must use living intellectuals, famous critical thinkers are the best. The derivative work acquires commercial value from their lack of commercial interest in value. So get Antonio Negri if you can. The *Dis* people had to settle for me as I come a lot cheaper.

An artwork can of course be a derivative of previous works of art, but a certain boredom is settling on this well-worn method, which in the end delights nobody but art historians, who become consultants to provenance as evaluators of quotation. The historians quote precedents so the gallerist may quote prices.

In any case, the apparent fact that the art market still sells works of art as things, as commodities also tends to mask the ways in which the artwork has changed. Works of art in our time are derivatives because that is how our economy works. In a previous era that prized manufacturing, works of art were distinguished by their manufacturing

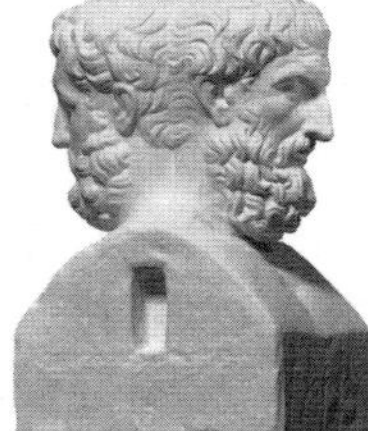

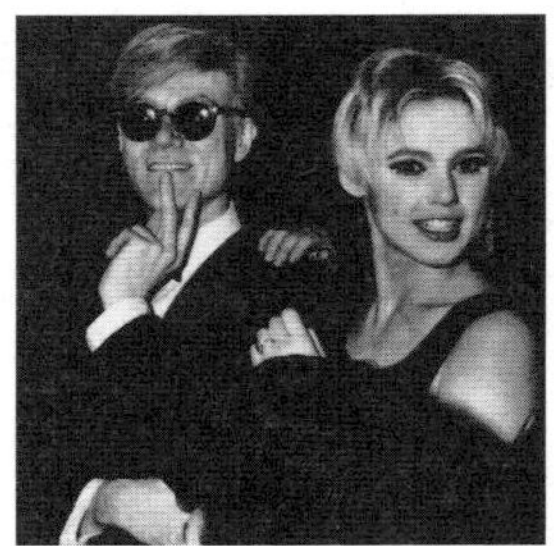

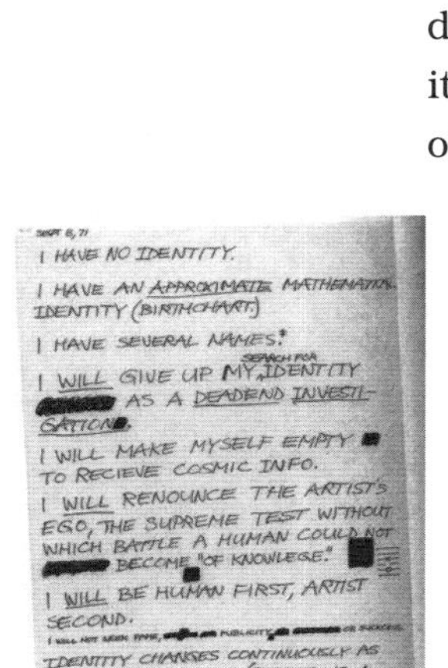

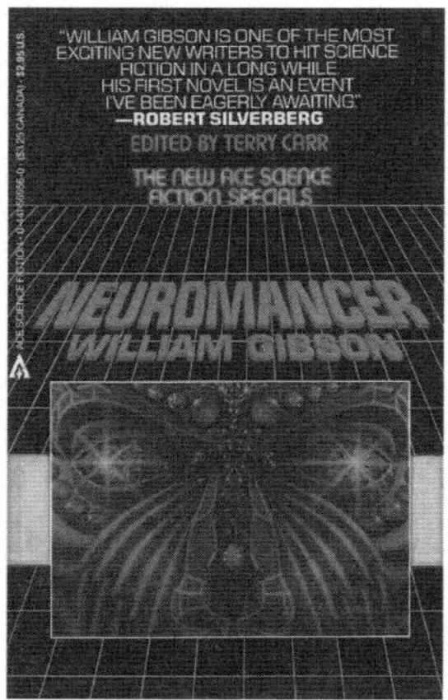

techniques. Thus, for example, works by impressionists, surrealists or so-called action painters could be treated as special, non-alienating commodities made by some other manufacturing process that took place other than in the workshop or on the assembly line.

This started to change in the sixties. Through Edie Sedgwick, Warhol discovered both how simulation could create provenance and how the work of art could be the derivative that would be a portfolio of simulation values. But it was perhaps minimalism's 'dematerialization of the work of art' that really put an end to the industrial model of art and paved the way for the birth of the financial model of art, of the work of art as a derivative that functions as a portfolio of simulation values. The work of art, like any other financial instrument, needs nothing to exist beyond its *documentation*.

The dematerialization of the work of art was not the dematerialization of the art worker. But one might speculate as to whether that might be the next step. Could the labour of art be automated? There was already a lovely image of this in William Gibson's novel *Neuromancer*, in which an artificial intelligence makes Joseph Cornell boxes that are if anything better than actual ones.

In short, then, I think what is most interesting about the relation between art and information is the reciprocity between art as rarity and information as ubiquity. It turns out that ubiquity can be a kind of distributed provenance, of which the work of art itself is the derivative. The work of art is then ideally a portfolio of different kinds of simulated value, the mixture of which can be a long-term hedge against the risks of various kinds of simulated value falling—such as the revelation of the name of a hidden artist, or the decline of the intellectual discourse on which the work depended, or the artist's falling into banality and over-production.

Since art became a special kind of financial instrument rather than a special kind of manufactured article, it has no longer needed to have a special means for its making, or even perhaps special makers. Indeed, curators now rival artists for influence must in the same way as DJs rival musicians. Both are a kind of portfolio manager of the qualitative. The next step after the dematerialization of the work of art may be the dematerialization of the art worker, whose place could be taken by new kinds of algorithmic function. These would still have to produce the range of simulations that might anchor the work of art as a derivative of their various kinds of sign value.

Originally presented at K-Art Conversations, Korea International Art Fair 2016. A slightly modified version also appeared in *e-flux Journal #77*, November 2016.

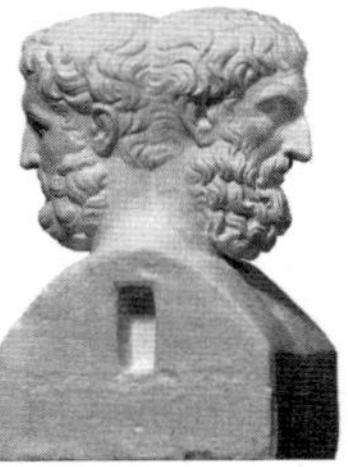

METHODS OF REPRESENTATION

Jazmina Figueroa

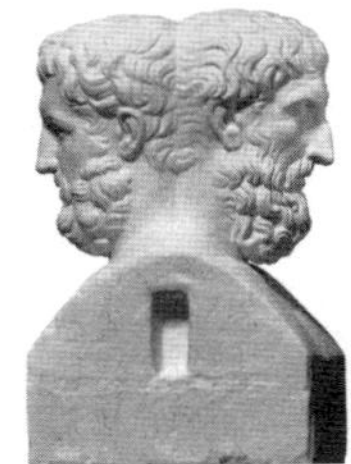

'I have long suspected that the vaunted 'freedom' to shed the markers of race and gender on the Internet is illusory, and that it masks a more disturbing phenomenon—the whitenizing of cyberspace.'
—Kali Tal[1]

Centring hegemonic experiences within technological developments entails the systemic erasure of the Other. Machines will always reflect the values of the societies they serve, and it is important to reject any dualism between physical and virtual spaces. The collection of data, and activities related to it, are one example of how hegemonic experiences are re-packaged as authentic experiences within an ideologically tendentious recasting of technological change as technological progress. In this paper, I will use three pillars of analysis to examine the lived experiences of integrated information economies: the first is the structural oppression of marginalized groups as they are confronted by technological developments; the second is hegemony[2] in relation to privacy, transparency and digital surveillance; and the third is comprised of authorship, or agency, and decentralisation as tools for representation within data sets and information technologies.

The race to quantify, collect, store, and model information by stakeholders of power, such as Internet corporations, results in the rapid development of digital infrastructures.[3] The rapidity of this development mirrors the ambitions of late liberalisms and adopts neo-colonial[4] approaches to the dissipation of information technologies with a white, cisgender, heteronormative, and able lens. In these digital infrastructures, information technologies are modelled as objective by the hegemonic identities that create, implement and control them. Examples where the development of these technologies lacked an intersection of the Other include the tagging of Asian people as blinking in photos taken by Nikon cameras,

1
Kali Tal, 'Life Behind the Screen', *Wired* October 1996, www.wired.com/1996/10/screen/.

2
By hegemony, I mean the manipulation by the dominant classes of the prevailing cultural values of a society with a view to continually inculcating in the other social classes a worldview that readily accommodates constant and opportunistically presented justifications for current social relations or versions of them, which in turn further the interest of the dominant classes—as though these relations were natural, go without saying, and so on.

3
Digital or computer infrastructures refers to the overlapping of networks, databases, algorithmic technologies, machine learning to automate the user experience of the Internet.

4
Phrases often used to describe advances in the field are similar to those used by settlers, such as 'digital frontier'.

the identification by Google Photo of black people as gorillas, and the tweeting of anti-Semitic, racist, and sexist statements by Microsoft's Tay Artificial Intelligence. In other examples—such as California's gang and criminal databases, which are based on bias caused in turn by the over-policing of disenfranchised neighbourhoods—the consequences are far more serious. And when social networks begin to demand and log the birth names of their trans users, it erases the lived experiences of those individuals—and those experiences become invisible.

There is not enough intersectional critique of the quantification of data structures and the commodification of the marginalized user. The erasure of the lived experiences of the Other allows marginalized groups to be held responsible for criticizing the repercussions, and violence, of these technological advances. In a 2016 article, *Transparency ≠ Accountability*, danah boyd emphasizes the importance of understanding accountability during algorithmic development: 'If we're going to deploy these systems, we need to articulate clearly what values we believe are important and then be held accountable for building systems to those standards.'[5]

In 2002, Les Back coined the term cyber-racism[6] to describe how racism is produced and distributed in virtual spaces. Back looks at instances of hate speech and of the distribution of white-supremacist messages. But in so doing, he fails to acknowledge the experience of racism as a systemic issue that is ingrained in western society with capitalist, neo-colonialist objectives. Back's examination of white-supremacist propaganda and activities online is a perpetuation of a narrative of racism as singular instances. The phenomenon of fascism as a product that racists consume is a consequence of neo-colonialist ideology, and may even serve as an apology for the current political-economic landscape. In

5
danah boyd, 'Transparency ≠ Accountability', *Data & Society: Points* 29 November 2016, `https://points.datasociety.net/transparency-accountability-3c04e4804504#.gcfpwu914`.

6
Les Back, 'Aryans Reading Adorno: Cyber-Culture and Twenty-First Century Racism', *Ethnic and Racial Studies* 25, no. 4 (2002), pp. 628–651.

7

Jill Lepore, 'What the Gospel of Innovation Gets Wrong.' *The New Yorker*, 6 May 2015.

8

Anthony Effinger, 'Andreessen on Finance: "We Can Reinvent the Entire Thing"' Bloomberg.com, 7 October 2014, www.bloomberg.com/news/articles/2014-10-07/andreessen-on-finance-we-can-reinvent-the-entire-thing--. Entrepreneur Marc Andreessen on Finance in *Bloomberg Magazine* states that the key to a successful financial technology is that, 'you want to do something so new and so different that the existing regulatory system doesn't know how to react to you. That is your window of opportunity'.

9

Joseph A. Schumpeter, *Capitalism, Socialism and Democracy* (Abingdon, 2013, 1st ed. 1942).

10

Irmgard Emmelhainz, 'Decolonization as the Horizon of Political Action', *e-flux Journal* 77 (November 2016), www.e-flux.com/journal/77/76637/decolonization-as-the-horizon-of-political-action/.

the United States, policy is put under a magnifying glass by marginalized groups after the 2017 inauguration but there is already evidence of a complacency towards racist, neo-colonialist infrastructures with the vast prison network and involvement in a global war industry worth billions.

The development of disruptive technologies also perpetuates the erasure of subjective experiences outside the hegemonic authentic. It is useful to note that the term disruptive is not equivalent to innovation, as Jill Lepore puts it, '*a theory of change founded on panic, anxiety, and shaky evidence.*'[7] Disruption also denotes technologies that are unmanageable by policy-makers and within corporatist and capitalist models today, thus reinforcing neoliberal ideologies and structures.[8] Joseph Schumpeter forecast the power of corporations over government in his 1942 book, *Capitalism, Socialism and Democracy*: technology, he wrote, would serve only to 'concentrate ownership and wealth towards large corporations'.[9] Post-colonial epistemology is an important expansion of this argument with Irmgard Emmelhainz's critique of colonial influence in technological development:

Modernity relies on critique to reinvent itself and to justify colonial exploitation, creating new hybrids and paradoxes and finding new ways to look at the world and our relationship to the past.[10]

Designers of Internet infrastructures exploit the data they collect on individuals through surveillance methods. Everything that happens online is collected and stored. These data sets cannot represent experiences beyond the hegemonic identities that create and implement them. The large-scale collection, storage, mining and deployment of data can be considered part of post-truth political discourse and practice, yet biased and uninformed conclusions presented by those involved in such activities are presented time and again as truthful or objective.

Modes of data collection mirror neo-colonialist thinking about knowledge and objectivity, as Paola Lopreiato writes:

> Western knowledge, culture and science, for centuries, were and sometimes still [are] focused on the study, analysis, understanding and description of the objective external world, separating it from the inner subjective world.[11]

11

Paola Lopreiato, 'Reflections on Art, Nature and Technology: The Role of Technology, Algorithm, Nature, Psyche and Imagination in the Aspiration of an Aesthetic Experience', *Technoetic Arts: A Journal of Speculative Research* 12, no. 2 (December 2014), pp. 423–428, doi: 10.1386/tear.12.2-3.423_1.

In *Confronting the Assumption of Whiteness in Virtual Spaces*—specifically haptic or sensory virtual-reality technologies—Kara Melton investigates how whiteness is experienced and developed for white-male centrality as the authentic virtual-reality experience: 'We must avoid thinking that this new virtual frontier is somehow separate from the violence and exclusions that shape the "outside world".'[12] Melton's analysis draws on the lived experience of touch for the user in the context of W. E. B. Du Bois's take on double consciousness:

> Through double consciousness, Du Bois argues that the subject and object exist simultaneously in the experience of black Americans, which means that the subject cannot be neutral in its lived experiences.[13]

12

Melton, Kara, 'Confronting the Assumption of Whiteness in Virtual Spaces', *Model View Culture Quarterly* no. 42 (19 October 2016), https://modelviewculture.com/pieces/confronting-the-assumption-of-whiteness-in-virtual-spaces.

13
Ibidem.

Melton also presents a series of questions for the future when subjectivity is considered in the development of haptic technologies. Subjectivity as a tool for representation also applies to methods of collecting data, why it is collected and who it is collected for, I have reframed Melton's questions so that they apply to data collection and algorithmic modelling:

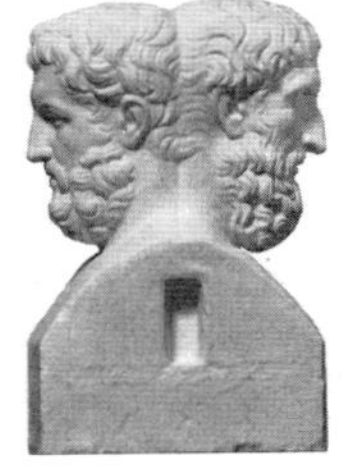

     METHODS OF REPRESENTATION

14
Melton describes a radicalised relationship to touch: 'The assumption of whiteness shapes who we can imagine having access to these virtual experiences, and, therefore, how we imagine we must build these experiences so that the user is fully immersed. In favor of producing seamless immersive experiences, that are not complicated by our varying, racialized relationships to touch, we seem to be losing sight of the truly complex mechanisms that produce it. When touch is understood only as a tool to produce immersive experiences, we lose sight of the real context of engagement: the lived experiences of the gameplayer. Even in virtual spaces touch is not contextless, and, more to the point, its only context is not the game. In this way, we should take pause when we begin to discuss touch and haptic experiences as if they can produce some sort of neutral reality.'

15
Julia Angwin, Jeff Larson and Terry Parris Jr., 'Breaking the Black Box: How Machines Learn to Be Racist', *ProPublica* 19 October 2016, `www.propublica.org/article/breaking-the-black-box-how-machines-learn-to-be-racist?word=Trump`.

1   How will algorithmic models positioned around the white male erase the experiences of marginalized people?

2   What assumptions about pattern-recognition design within data sets may result from these assumptions about whiteness?

3   What are the implications of recreating radicalized and violent hierarchies with predictive technologies, such radicalised relationships to commodification? What does this tell us about the future of these technologies?[14]

4   How are data sets in particular primed to recreate radicalized violence?

5   What can we learn about whiteness, for example as the default, by engaging with the ways it is centred in the development of our technologies?

ProRepublica's episodic research on machine bias in 2016 provided a lot of evidence about why and how machines 'learn to be racist'.[15] Because algorithmic models are opaque—the phenomenon is known as the black box—evidence to support the modelling of biases into algorithms is circumstantial, and research projects such as Mimi Onuoha's *Missing Data Sets* are crucial to understanding the ways in which the modelling of pattern-recognition technologies may not be comprehensive enough. The project is a GitHub repository highlighting data sets that are missing but that should exist if subjectivity is to be considered central to the development of these technologies. This list of data sets that are incomplete or missing reveals social biases and indifferences to collecting certain types of information.[16]

Onuoha writes

This list will always be incomplete, and is designed to be illustrative rather than comprehensive:

16
Mimi Onuoha, 'On Miss-
ing Data Sets', *GitHub*,
3 February 2016,
https://github.com/
MimiOnuoha/missing-
data sets.

* Civilians killed in encounters with police or law enforcement agencies
* Sales and prices in the art world (and relationships between artists and gallerists)
* People excluded from public housing because of criminal records
* Trans people killed or injured in instances of hate crime
* Poverty and employment statistics that include people who are behind bars
* Muslim mosques/communities surveilled by the FBI/CIA
* Mobility for older adults with physical disabilities or cognitive impairments
* LGBT older adults discriminated against in housing
* Undocumented immigrants currently incarcerated and/or underpaid
* Undocumented immigrants for whom prosecutorial discretion has been used to justify release or general punishment
* Measurements for global web users that take into account shared devices and VPNs
* True measures around how often sexual harassment happens in the workplace
* Firm statistics on how often police arrest women for making false rape reports
* Caucasian children adopted by parents of color
* Total number of local and state police departments using stingray phone trackers (IMSI-catchers)

Through this project, Onuoha concludes that methods of data collection are always subjective, whether individual or hegemonic subjectivity is involved:

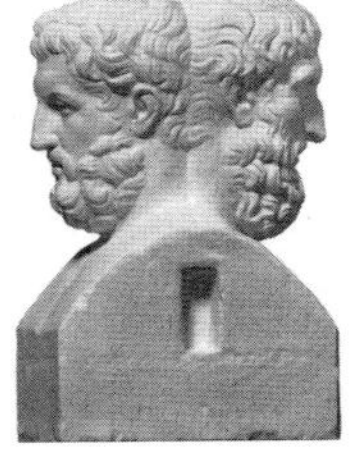

There's no pure objectivity encoded into data sets. Each one is the

 METHODS OF REPRESENTATION

17
Mimi Onuoha, 'The Point of Collection', *Data & Society: Points* 31 October 2016, `https://points. datasociety.net/the-point-of-collection-8ee44ad7c2fa#.5lt5w5yga.`

18
Kaveh Waddell, 'America Already Had a Muslim Registry', *The Atlantic*, 20 December 2016, `www.theatlantic. com/technology/ archive/2016/12/ america-already-had-a-muslim-registry/511214/.`

19
Matt Cagle, 'Facebook, Instagram, and Twitter Provided Data Access for a Surveillance Product Marketed to Target Activists of Color', *ACLU of Northern California*, 11 October 2016, `www.aclunc.org/blog/ facebook-instagram-and-twitter-provided-data-access-surveillance-product-marketed-target.`

20
Spencer Woodman, 'Documents Suggest Palantir Could Help Power Trump's "Extreme Vetting" of Immigrants', *The Verge*, 21 December 2016, `www.theverge. com/2016/12/21/ 14012534/palantir-peter-thiel-trump-immigrant-extreme-vetting.`

result of a number of human processes and decisions that affect, in a variety of ways, the data that they aim to report. In this sense, the moment of data collection starts before any data is actually produced.[17]

Based on this assessment, Onuoha advances four reasons for the non-existence of these data sets:

1 Those who have the resources to collect data lack the incentive to…
2 The data to be collected resist simple quantification (corollary: we prioritize collecting things that fit our modes of collection)…
3 The act of collection involves more work than the benefit the presence of the data is perceived to give…
4 There are advantages to nonexistence.

Information is collected for a purpose, and Onuoha also highlights the advantages of non-existence when it comes to ensuring the safety of individuals: it can help that information is not collected or stored. For example, there are plenty intrinsically violent forms of data collection in the current political landscape, such as a Muslim registry,[18] tracking social-media alliances to the Black Lives Matter movement,[19] and immigrant databases[20]. An article published by *Rewire* in January 2017 lists already-existing US government systems, such as databases of driver's licenses, that could have information extracted from them to 'hasten mass deportation efforts if used against immigrant communities'.[21]

The Critical Art Ensemble's (CAE) Swipe project was a performance and workshop to raise awareness of 'Automatic Identification and Data Capture (AIDC) technologies and draw attention to some of the related social implications.'[22] When someone would purchase a drink at the bar, they would receive a receipt containing all the information CAE was able to extract from their driver's license with any personal information CAE could harvest from other online databases:

> The workshop offers a demonstration that demystifies the data collection and data warehouse businesses, offering a behind-the-scenes look at the Swipe bar. The Web site, launched in February 2004, offers a set of hands-on tools for the motivated cultural activist. On the Web site, users can decipher the two-dimensional barcode on a driver's license through downloadable program, determine the value of personal information on the open market using a data calculator, and request a data file from big data warehouses … . Using a bulletin board system, users can post how many errors appear in their requested files and keep track of the response time of the data warehouses to correction requests.

The Swipe project illustrates how an individual's data, stored within governmental or corporate systems, might be flawed. This implies that using that date for other purposes can have dangerous consequences. CAE's intention with the Swipe project was to raise awareness and understanding of AIDC and to provide a critique of 'a broad range of data surveillance activities'.[23] When information is collected, distributed and stored, where is the control? How is that control audited, and based on what ethical system or principles? Recently, EPIC, the Electronic Privacy Information Centre, called for algorithm designers to make their data sources and profiles transparent as a way of improving 'the models engineered into machine learning technologies and Artificial Intelligence'.[24] To reiterate boyd's point, which I cited above: there may be no advantage to having transparent algorithmic models,

21

Tina Vasquez, 'Here Are the State and Federal Databases That Could Hurt Immigrant Communities in Trump's Administration', *Rewire*, 11 January 2017, https://rewire.news/article/2017/01/11/state-federal-databases-hurt-immigrant-communities-trump-administration/.

22

Jamie Schulte and Brooke Singer, 'Surveillance Creep! New Manifestations of Data Surveillance at the Beginning of the Twenty-First Century', *Radical History Review* 95 (2006), pp. 70–88.

23

Ibidem.

24

'EPIC Promotes "Algorithmic Transparency" at Annual Meeting of Privacy Commissioners', https://epic.org/2016/10/epic-promotes-algorithmic-tran.html, 20 October 2016.

because systemic issues, such as erasure, and the socio-technical issues they create should be accounted for in the ethics of algorithmic development.[25]

One appealing case for transparency through models of decentralization as an operational tool is to preserve identity or authorship within online networks and establish individual autonomy and agency. For example, Blockchain is the technology behind digital currencies such as Bitcoin. Because of the decentralized and cryptographic nature of blockchains, digital assets can be owned and transferred. The prospect of individual ownership of data outside institutionalized entities is an exciting one that inspires ideas of complete transparency and control over the self as data; how the self operates within virtual networked spaces; or how one is profiled or represented in pattern-recognition models. But what are the actions one can take if they gain ownership of their data?

In relationship to the discourses around erasure and preserving representation, agency and autonomy are equally political choices. Authorship can be an instrument for creating alliances with counter-public identities, especially those that have, historically, been commodified. There is a compromise between choosing privacy or being transparent for the sake of representation, but was the privilege of opting out or resisting ever accessible to the Other? Through technological erasure in the post-digital age, the authentic experience of marginalized bodies can be understood as a dual experience—both being the commodity and embodying the community.

I can only look to subjective accounts from peers and others invested in the representation of marginalized identities in online networks. A shared sentiment is reflected in a personal account of online visibility for immigrant families by Zara Rahman: 'My mother wants me to balance visibility and privacy, so our extended family members can see the young woman I've become, but not the extent of my "westernization".'[26]

25
Mike Ananny and Kate Crawford, 'Seeing Without Knowing: Limitations of the Transparency Ideal and Its Application to Algorithmic Accountability', *New Media & Society* 13 December 2016, doi: 10.1177/1461444816676645.

26
Zara Rahman, 'Close Calls', *Real Life Magazine*, 26 January 2017, http://reallifemag.com/close-calls/.

Secondary Sources

Bassett, Nathanael Edward. 'The Private and the Public: Identity and Politics in Virtual Space.' Presented at Media in Transition 8, 5 May 2013, www.academia.edu/1567245/The_Private_and_the_Public_Identity_and_Politics_in_Virtual_Space.

Freire, Paulo. *Pedagogy of the Oppressed*. London, etc., 2000.

Hall, Stuart. *Representation: Cultural Representations and Signifying Practices*. London: 1997.

Dahlberg, Lincoln. 'Re-constructing Digital Democracy: An Outline of Four "Positions".' *New Media & Society* 7, no. 2 (2011), pp. 855–872, doi: 1461444810389569.

Daniels, Jessie. 'Cloaked Websites: Propaganda, Cyber-Racism and Epistemology in the Digital Era.' *New Media & Society* 11, no. 5 (2009), pp. 659–683.

Daniels, Jessie. 'Race and Racism in Internet Studies: A Review and Critique.' *New Media & Society* 15, no. 5 (2013), pp. 695–719.

Steyerl, Hito, and Kate Crawford. 'Data Streams.' *The New Inquiry*, 23 January 2017, http://thenewinquiry.com/features/data-streams/.

Floridi, Luciano, and Mariarosaria Taddeo. 'What is Data Ethics?' *Philosophical Transactions of the Royal Society A: Mathematical, Physical and Engineering Sciences* 374, no. 2083 (2016), doi: 10.1098/rsta.2016.0360.

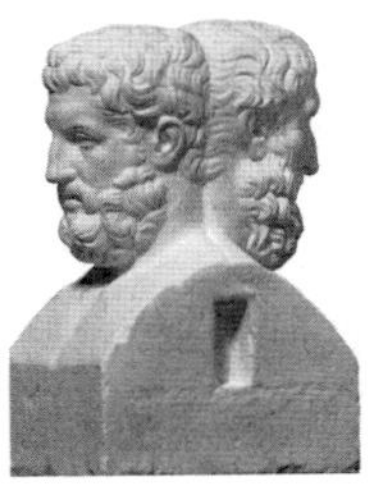

ACHIEVING AGENCY IN THE FACE OF TECHNOLOGY
Interview with Holly Herndon and Mat Dryhurst

Barbara Cueto & Bas Hendrikx

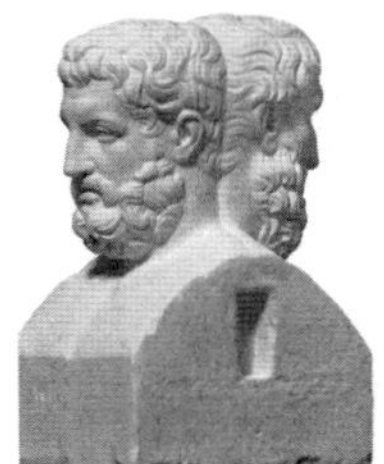

BARBARA CUETO & BAS HENDRIKX
Digital advocacy is becoming more apparent in projects you have both done, not just when it comes to generating awareness around topics such as digital rights or the politics behind the online distribution of information, but also in terms of creating actual tools. You seem to be concerned with the infrastructure of artistic production, networks, and distribution platforms. Could you explain this in light of your recent projects?

MAT DRYHURST
We are quite candid with the people around us, and we've had the good fortune to have many opportunities to see quite deeply into different cultural infrastructures over the past few years. It makes some sense to report that back through the work we do. If we make something for the recorded-music industry, we spend time thinking about the affordances and opportunities to experiment with that platform, and so on. Those who find some success within a cultural profession have a unique opportunity to reflect those findings back to people—though they also arguably have the most to lose in translating what they see and experience.

The design of a platform or network communicates implicit expectations for what you are supposed to do, and not supposed to do, and that open up new frontiers for the exploration of what experimentation means. In music, I think we have collectively done about as much as can be done with a linear composition distributed on wax or waveform. The new opportunity is in designing our own conditions for how the music is received and understood, and expanding the agency of artists to make gestures in these new conditions—gestures that will break rules and connect with people.

HOLLY HERNDON
We want people to have agency in their lives, and that means getting involved in the infrastructures that contribute to our daily behaviour. The first step towards achieving agency is understanding these infrastructures—and we both still

have a lot to learn. We need to have clear ideas about what we want these platforms to be and either build them ourselves or determine principles for the platforms we want to participate in, and support those that meet that criteria.

BC & BH

Post-truth was the word of the year, uncertainty seems to be our zeitgeist, and the power of social media has become even more pervasive in the last months of 2016. Holly, in your song Unequal, you repeat 'To change the shape of our future, to be unafraid, to break away … A louder fight, a harder fight'. Mat, your project SAGA encourages users to avoid third-party services to host and distribute songs or files, so that they can reclaim ownership of their work. Do you each consider your work as a call to action? In your opinion, how can we step out of the comfort zone of social media and respond to the current situation? And what tools could we use to do this?

HOLLY HERNDON

I co-wrote *Unequal* with Colin Self a few years ago. We both wanted to speak to the racial and gender inequities we were witnessing, so in a way it was a call for action. The musical palette of that piece was inspired by feudal Europe, as a metaphor about current digital rights and our relationships with platforms. I used the palette in 2014 in a mix with Swiss journalist Hannes Grassegger for DIS. Our data is mined with no compensation, we can be banished from platforms for any reason, and we do not have the choice not to participate without incurring serious social and economic consequences. This is a serious class issue, and worth calling attention to. Doreen St. Felix wrote an article in the *Fader*, which I highly recommend, entitled 'Black Teens Are Breaking the Internet and Seeing None of the Profits'.[1] Mat's SAGA project speaks directly to these kinds of issues. Many of them are intertwined, and we feel best equipped to tackle them from this angle.

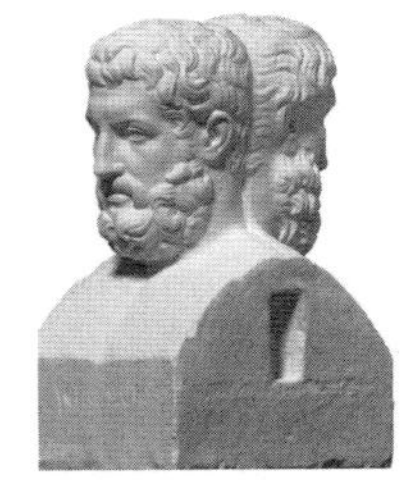

1

Doreen St. Felix, 'Black Teens Are Breaking the Internet and Seeing None of the Profits'. *Fader*, December 2015, www.thefader.com/2015/12/03/on-fleek-peaches-monroee-meechie-viral-vines.

 ACHIEVING AGENCY IN THE FACE OF TECHNOLOGY

MAT DRYHURST
SAGA does encourage people to reclaim ownership, and goes farther by making each instance of a work online a unique opportunity to express oneself. This web-site-specific approach expands the possibility of what a work can do, and could also be deployed as a strategy to address the dissemination of false information. For example, not long ago I saw a plea from the scientific community for a tool that allows scientists to comment on the misuse of scientific facts in articles. The logic of SAGA could address this, as it would allow for scientists to respond to the misuse of their work in every discrete location in which it has been distorted. This is not just a call for, but a means to, action.

Post-truth is an interesting concept, as it implies that we previously had a system of truth. I reject that implication. The coming to power of figures such as Trump is a symptom of a larger deceitful and manipulative political and economic system that has been in place for decades. Commercial interests have distorted the truth for as long as I have been alive, and we can see that showing up in purportedly objective political and journalistic coverage of issues over time. Google and Facebook are advertising networks. Their implicit goal is to sell you on something, irrespective of whether it is true. I think a big leap would be a movement to socialize these technologies, and to try to restore some semblance of truth and progress outside privatized commercial logics.

BC & BH
Many artists refer to their work in terms of questioning or critiquing, yet your work seems geared towards finding new solutions and answers. There is a certain level of optimism in your approach. Could your work be perceived as a form of empowerment?

MAT DRYHURST
I do hope that the things that we do create space and encouragement for others, but to be honest I am sceptical of strategies that place ideas such as 'empowerment' at the centre, because that term has become synonymous with

neoliberal-marketing jargon. I think we need to take the concept of power seriously, and not be seduced by the kind of power that the market offers us. For instance, I don't see successful people within the entertainment industry as powerful: while they may make a lot of money, and have a platform to speak from, their power depends largely on their advocacy of an ultimately disempowering system of exploitation, illusions and competition. This is why new alternatives need to come to be, and why people need to get wise to the permissions afforded by the structures they participate in.

This kind of approach makes me feel a little isolated as an artist. For example, I joke about Saga that it would be easier to find funding and support for the project if I had made a speculative film with cool fonts about the possibility of its existence, rather than building software that actually works and implicitly demonstrates an alternative. I think that one reason for this is that within the art world infrastructure people are largely encouraged to speculate on the possibility of alternatives, and there is little incentive to enact these. Many of the most 'empowered' artists within that infrastructure are simply creating interesting conversational diversions to decorate and legitimize a powerful and conservative transactional art system; they are kept around as a marketing device of sorts. That is not power. Questioning and critique are essential in the formation of new ideas. However, the objective ought to be to enact something better—and people with power generally don't like to give it up. I'm optimistic about our ability to form these new structures, but I am increasingly sober about how difficult it might be to realize them fully.

HOLLY HERNDON

I see a difference between agency and empowerment. Feeling free to act as you like is different from being given the opportunity to do so. I don't think that art has to necessarily do anything, it's free to be whatever it wants, but that's also a wonderful opportunity: if it can be anything it wants, it seems like a missed opportunity for it to not attempt to do something.

I was raised in the US south, in a deeply religious community, where optimism runs deep as an embedded aspect of the worldview. While my outlook has dramatically changed since leaving that part of the world, the optimism is difficult to shake. :) Given the current political climate, it is sometimes difficult to maintain that approach, but it's an important aspect, particularly in the realm of creativity. We have an abundance of dystopian perspectives, although many of those seem outmoded and borne of another time. Rather than updating a dystopian art context, why not use that same energy to try to present collective fantasies? Art does not operate, or is not received, in isolation from other aspects of culture. Many of the projects we have done, for example, have attracted interest from people who are better placed to address some of the issues we care about, and have opened opportunities to work towards something different. Trends in politics and technology have been pointing towards negative outcomes for some time, and so it has always been the focus to be positively critical.

BC & BH

Our digital 'domestic' spaces are less private than they may seem, and they are becoming increasingly politicized. Can we use a collective acknowledgement of this to our advantage? Is a reconfiguration possible?

<u>MAT DRYHURST</u>

I hope so, but it's hard. It's like getting people to acknowledge a drug habit. I refer to Facebook, for example, as a 'dopamine dealer': even when people are aware they have a problem it is still incredibly hard to kick it, when your livelihood and social relations depend—as they often do—on participation. My hope is that attempting to generate awareness and come up with alternatives will gradually encourage people to start moving away from this participation. You see it happening more and more with secure-messaging platforms, and hopefully that can expand to all aspects of life. It may be that they are too powerful, seductive and supported by state bodies—it's like a mechanized version of the Narcissus fable, where people fall so strongly in love with an environment constructed in their own image that they lose the will to live outside it. I mention state support, as I also believe that this is an important factor: I don't expect the average person on the street to solve this problem or put their careers or lives at risk by defecting, but I do expect governments to have the foresight to see the havoc these techno-structures play on people's sense of well-being and purpose. I think there is a correlation between austerity, economic depression and the growing dependence on these platforms, and that in most cases the state is happy for the public to be placated and policed by the expectations of their own communities. The reconfiguration, ultimately, would be most effective on a state level.

BC & BH

Geert Lovink asserts in his essay *On Social Media Ideology*[2] that social media must be considered an ideology, since they have become infrastructural and bind together

> media, culture, and identity into an ever-growing cultural performance... . [A]ll of this imbricated with the entrepreneurial values of venture capital and start-up culture, with their underside of declining livelihoods and growing inequality.

How would you relate to this statement?

MAT DRYHURST

Different platforms represent competing ideologies—fiefdoms—where you are afforded certain freedoms in exchange for your compliance. Apple, for example, takes your privacy seriously. However, in exchange you are not allowed to leave their proprietary walled garden. Google, on the

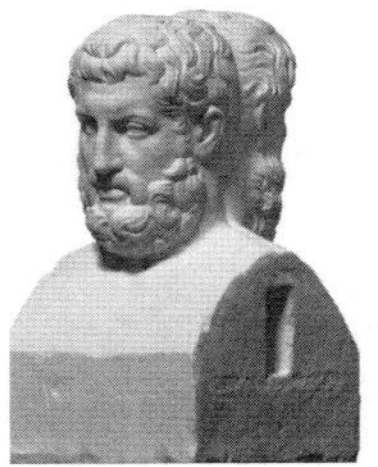

2

Geert Lovink, 'On Social Media Ideology', *e-flux Journal #75* (September 2016).

other hand, encourages you to explore freely, and follows closely behind you, collecting and reselling the data that you generate. They all represent ideologies, and most perpetuate those ideologies in using them to the desired effect.

HOLLY HERNDON

The design of platforms is inherently political, and our adherence to its logics represents ideological compliance. It is troubling how much of this infrastructure is ostensibly dictated by the interests of the advertising industry, for example. There will always be examples of groups' using such infrastructures to good ends, but ultimately the design and financial objectives set the parameters for how much you can accomplish. I don't see the current dominant social media platforms as permanent. To this end, we've started to hold community meetings in our space to brainstorm small interventions that could take place to move people away.

MAT DRYHURST

Yes, for example, we held a meeting not long ago trying to think of an effective way to move people off Facebook events—as it appears that is the one thing holding people back from leaving. In many cases the design of these things is not the biggest barrier, more just finding the resources to maintain alternatives. The fact that the arts do not have an easy way to access the means to support alternative platforms, for example, also communicates an ideology. Our communities ought to be the first people taking this on!

BC & BH

In your song Locker Leak, you refer to a whole array of products from yoga to aloe vera entwined in slogans of advertising campaigns. Why is it relevant for you to mention the consumption of these kind of products and activities? In the same vein in your song Lonely at the Top, you use typical ASMR sounds[3] as a coping strategy for the extremely wealthy to justify their status, a 'therapy for the 1%', as you mentioned. How to do you relate to the politics of privilege intrinsically related to them?

3 Editor's note: Autonomous sensory meridian response (ASMR) is a euphoric experience characterized by a tingling sensation on the skin that typically begins on the scalp and moves down the back of the neck and upper spine, facilitating relaxation. It has been compared with auditory-tactile synesthesia, and there is a large YouTube community for its videos.

HOLLY HERNDON

Locker Leak was a collaboration with the artist Spencer Longo, who was using Twitter as a venue for word sculptures; is it necessary to make assemblages of objects, or could they simply be invoked with words, bypassing the arduous marketplace? Spencer wrote the text, and he writes that he was thinking of those intimate moments online when you are hovering over the Buy button on Amazon, and being tracked as they try to learn your habits to better market to you. I had an interesting conversation with a young veterinarian from Poland about this track. He loved the lyric: Be the first of your friends to like Greek yoghurt this summer. With so much creative work emulating consumer culture, I could see his confusion as to whether consumerism was being glorified, or being encouraged. I think that exercise was intended more as an acknowledgment of a state of mind—a common bind. It's more like comedy.

Perhaps the critique is clearer on *Lonely at the Top*, which targets the 1% with ASMR self-help language. While I think parody can be cathartic, ultimately it's more powerful to evoke an alternative aesthetic altogether. With *Lonely at the Top*, Claire Tolan and I were both interested in the real intimacy and care that happen in the ASMR community, where, for example, the comment sections are designed so that almost all text is supportive. This is perhaps not realistic or even optimal for the wider Internet, but still interesting to see a section carved out like this for kindness.

BC & BH

The digital sphere comes with a certain set of rules and behaviours. How does the digital world influence your experiences? Is there any difference for you between the virtual and physical worlds? And what, in your opinion, is an authentic experience?

MAT DRYHURST

That is a huge question! In short, the dig-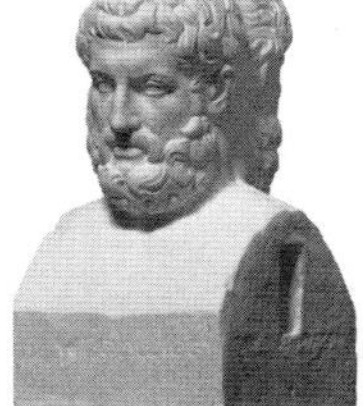
ital world modulates your experience of

     ACHIEVING AGENCY IN THE FACE OF TECHNOLOGY

the physical world, and its ubiquity and its enmeshment with all aspects of our lives mean that it is very difficult to make clean distinctions between the virtual and the physical as concepts— just as it might be difficult to make clean distinctions between the mind and the body. I don't necessarily believe in pure experience, or at least I think that an entanglement with tools and technology is such a part of the modern human brain that we cannot fathom such a state. I feel that everyone has different anchors by which they orient their sense of authenticity. The easiest anchor, perhaps, is the reactionary rejection of new modes of experience as inauthentic. There is also, at the other extreme, the thirsty desire for accelerated progress as some kind of marker of authenticity of the collective human condition—the sometimes pseudo-religious Transhuman position on artificial intelligence, for example. I sympathize more with the latter, but at my core I am a humanist and derive authenticity from implicitly human moments within an environment of accelerating change. Timely humour, for example, is one of my anchors for authenticity. This debate will get a lot crazier once bots can indiscernibly make a good joke without exposing themselves as bots.

BC & BH

In your work you often use your own data as a source on which to build. You've used the term boomeranging to describe, for instance, the transformation of your web-browsing into sound. Could you tell us a bit more about what you call *Net-Concrète*?

MAT DRYHURST

That was a term we used internally for a system I designed around 2012. At the time, I was trying to make a piece of music to communicate my general anxiety about juggling jobs and not feeling as if I had the time to fully realize the thing I wanted, so I made a tool to track what I was browsing at work and form crude compositions out of that audio— thus making that time at work for me, so to speak. It ended up assuming a different life when we started thinking

AUTHENTICITY?

about surveillance, and in a sense provided a pretty fitting palette for the formation of a lot of the work that led to *Platform,* because it successfully communicates some of the abstract coherence of the browsing experience. The *musique concrète* analogy is quite direct, inasmuch as it abstracts these sounds from their original context and assumes some agency and some creative licence over them. Schaeffer's[4] form of sampling represented some form of modernity—the original concrète experiments reconciled and translated—were emblematic of—a new era of tape recorders and accessible microphone technology, just as digital samplers later came to be iconic of a state of ubiquitous digital technology were everywhere in the seventies and eighties. If anything, this technique works as an attempt to processthe common experience of incessant, unavoidable streams of sound and to make a gesture amidst all that noise. In a way, it helps for the music to occupy its own space: the voice is written to find a place within the clutter rather than to be drowned out by it.

4
Editors' note: Pierre Schaeffer is a French composer known for his avant-garde *music concrète,* an experimental technique of musical composition that records sounds as raw material.

BC & BH

In your music, you utilize everyday sounds, from a blender to tones from your phone, thus generating an almost posthuman approach to music-making. Where do you position your music? How do you relate it to musique concrète, for example? What do you think are the new challenges in terms of composition?

HOLLY HERNDON

I'm not sure how to place it. Hopefully it belongs to today and reflects our time.

We unashamedly use our laptops, and try to find unique processes that reflect the idea for the song whenever we can. I'm not concerned to have sound be alienated from its source, as with *musique concrète.* I actually like the connection to the physical world. Making the digital and the

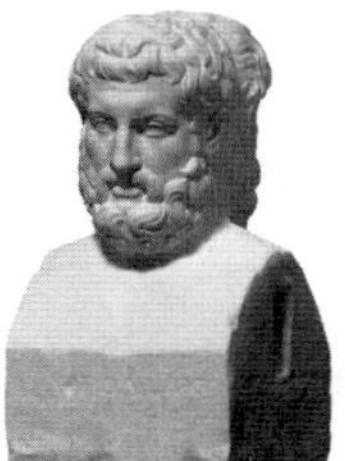

     ACHIEVING AGENCY IN THE FACE OF TECHNOLOGY

physical work together instead of creating distinct layers is a long-term goal. It also just makes sense to use the sounds that we live with every day. We aren't in an industrial era: there aren't abandoned buildings around us to bang on, and most of the fundamental changes occurring are abstracted through these personal devices, so it makes sense to experiment with those devices.

Some challenges strictly in terms of composition, besides infrastructural challenges around releasing music, might be maintaining cultural relevance when the music industry is increasingly homogenizing with the advertising and lifestyle industry, navigating the challenge of fixed media vs fluid media, and competing with music composed by machines. Everything we do is tied to reflecting our imperfect lives and emotional and intellectual opinions, which perhaps is some way to future-proof ourselves!

MAT DRYHURST

As for challenges within composition, I agree with most of what Holly says. The AI thing is interesting: if your music is boring enough to be automated by a machine, you won't need to be doing it in ten years. I also think that centrism and commercialism are big problems, because we are in this weird moment where traditionally marginalized music has found a new audience, and has begun to assimilate with capital in ways we haven't seen before. While that has presented opportunities for some, it presents a significant challenge, as many of the strategies and sounds that were developed for specific needs and communities become assimilated into the centrist soup. A lot of fields have this problem, and it is a sometimes lonely but essential pursuit to experiment and be critical in the same spirit that gave us those aesthetic ruptures in the first place. I watched a Mark Fisher talk a while back where he discussed the deep psychedelic component to pop music, where you expected artists to get more experimental the larger they got, and that implicitly represented a form of collective possibility for the public. With few exceptions, I don't see many examples of that within contemporary music, and that is a challenge.

Music, especially electronic music, comes with a well-defined and static set of rules, where, for instance, the DJ is located in an almost religious position with regard to the public—as though on an altar or in a pulpit. In your concerts, you try to subvert this by interacting with the audience, but also by writing to them. Why do you create this kind of ambiance? Why do you think it is necessary to structure your interactions this way?

<u>HOLLY HERNDON</u>

We're both interested in digital intimacy, and in establishing new archetypes for what we do. We are drawn to the power of live music, of sharing time and space with an audience. This is, for the most part, quite different from most people's conceptions of DJing. In a live performance, I feel as though so much more can go wrong, and that there are different affordances and expectations: you have far more means to communicate, and you can establish a narrative so that it becomes a kind of theatre. We want the show to be human and candid. It's different from the traditional front-person hype role. The text and the transparency represent a kind of mediated intimacy that illustrates our point that our digital selves are real and intimate parts of our physical selves. We also try to be approachable and, in the end, to have fun on stage. I come from a rather serious electronic-music background, but that doesn't really fit my personality. As a woman, I also recognize that there are different expectations for what I am supposed to be on stage, so I try to ignore these, and that's not always easy. I feel like that is an important infrastructure to subvert: when I was growing up, I was often alienated from the representations of women I saw in front of me. The live stage is a powerful symbolic place, and I take it as a responsibility to make our live shows representative of our politics

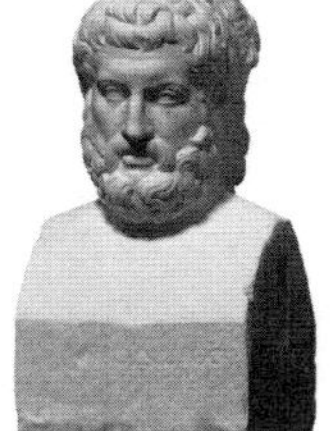

and our personalities. It is not always successful, but that is also an important dimension to the show. I want it to feel like anything could happen, and to remind people that we are in fact there together.

<u>MAT DRYHURST</u>

We have been involved in music for a long time, and I honestly feel as though I can tell from the first ten seconds what most shows are going to look and sound like. So as well as all the interesting stuff, we experiment with the live show to retain our own interest. The live text is something we have done for a long time, as one really simple way to create a connection with people. It has an improv-comedy angle, which I think is really powerful in opposition to most of the canned playback or posturing I witness at shows. For a while I used to make plays based on text messages about the exact audience in the room, by spying on them all beforehand and using that to inform the narrative. For a while we also published our personal numbers, and I still occasionally get text messages from people from shows years ago. I refer to these aspects of performance as 'Turing Texts'—basically something to communicate that there is a live, vulnerable, human on stage prone to typos and occasional bad jokes. The live aspect has deeper implications too: I have deep-seated mistrust of the push towards seamless experience in our everyday lives. Live performances are among the few opportunities we have to be there in real time with one another, and yet the trend has been moving towards some weird automated kick-drum spectacle with trippy polygons for a long time now. It's a problem.

The other aspect to these performances is that, by using the space behind us as a billboard to communicate ideas, we are also using the social media feeds of audience members to spread political messaging. It's, again, a matter of agency over our practice. When an audience member takes a picture of our show, as sometimes happens, they are boosting the signal of a message we wanted to see in the world. It perhaps comes across as naive in contrast to the impressive spectacles many others put on, but there is a logic to it. It's engaging consistent with our ideals, and it makes for a far better picture. :)

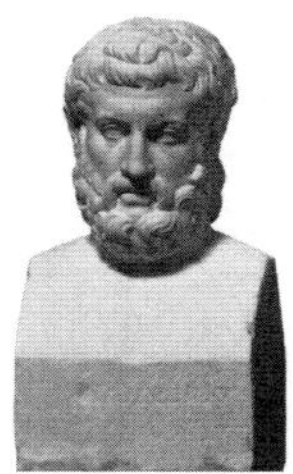

TRAP OF IDENTITY AND DELUSION OF TRUTH

Franco 'Bifo' Berardi

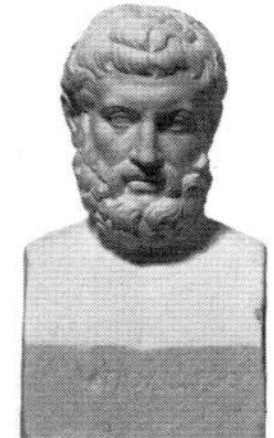

My theory is that identity consists of two contradictory imperatives. … There's the imperative
to keep secrets and the imperative to have them
known. How do you know that you're a person, distinct from other people? By keeping certain things
to yourself. You guard them inside, because if you
don't, there's no distinction between inside and
outside. Secrets are the way you know you even
have an inside. A radical exhibitionist is a person
who has forfeited his identity… Your identity exists
at the intersection of these lines of trust.

[T]he terrors of technocracy, which sought to liber-
ate humanity from its humanness through the effi-
ciency of markets and the rationality of machines.
This was the truly eternal fixture of illegitimate
revolution, this impatience with irrationality, this
wish to be clean of it once and for all.
—Jonathan Franzen[1]

1
Jonathan Franzen, *Purity:
A Novel* (New York, 2015),
p. 275 and p. 450.

The concept of authenticity refers to a pre-mediated
experience, but the pre-mediated experience does not
exist and has never existed. It is just a delusion of purity.
Nevertheless, it's clear that in the digital sphere the layers of mediation have grown enormously thick and dense,
thus enhancing the perception of inauthenticity to the
point of pathology.

'Be yourself' is the suggestion that we receive from advertising discourse. The tough part is that you don't know
who your self is, because it is the product of the mutually
contradictory injunctions that are thus advertised and that
push you in different directions.

You are at the point of intersection of countless semiotic
flows that stimulate your attention and your perception of
the self. This means that, like identity, authenticity is a
pseudo-concept. It does not define something that exists
in itself. Rather, it idolizes an illusion. Nevertheless, the

sense of inauthenticity, of the loss of identity, is real in the contemporary subconscious, in the suffering self-perception of this precarious generation.

Authenticity, then, does not exist—but the longing for it is real. The retrospective nostalgic idolization of an authentic condition is quite real, even if the condition itself isn't. The idolization is the effect of the present malaise. The current debate about post-truth, which exploded in the international press after the victory of Trump, is based in the double bind of authenticity.

Post-Truth and the Exhaustion of the Critical Mind

Donald J. Trump's supporters were probably heartened in September, when, according to an article shared nearly a million times on Facebook, the candidate received an endorsement from Pope Francis. Their opinions on Hillary Clinton may have soured even further after reading a Denver Guardian article that also spread widely on Facebook, which reported days before the election that an F.B.I. agent suspected of involvement in leaking Mrs. Clinton's emails was found dead in an apparent murder-suicide. There is just one problem with these articles: they were completely fake.[2]

2
Zeynep Tufekci, 'Mark Zuckerberg is in Denial', *New York Times*, 17 November 2016.

Commentators and politicians have blamed the increasing unreliability of the media, denouncing the effects that false information is having on political life.

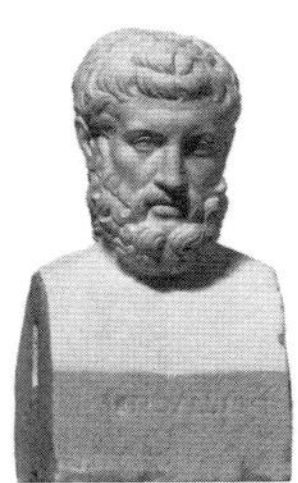

The panic about fake news has given fuel to the idea that we live in a 'post-truth' era. The Oxford English Dictionary has even made post-truth its 'word of the year', defining it as 'circumstances in which objective facts are less influential in shaping public opinion than appeals to emotion and personal belief.' But just as with fake news, the truth, if I may still use that word, about post-truth is more complex than many allow.[3]

3
Kenan Malik, 'Gatekeepers and the Rise of Fake News', *New York Times*, 4 December 2016.

All the buzz about post-truth, and the angry claim for the re-establishment of truth in the public discourse, are based on ignorance of what power is in a scenario in which info-stimuli are intensified, and where noise and confusion prevail. Democracy used to be based on a critical discrimination between true and false, and on rational determination. A decision was an act of conscious selection based on the slow examination of a finite number of enunciations. The acceleration of the information flow, and the intensification of the nervous stimuli, have changed the nature of decision-making and of politics in general.

In the digital age, power is no longer the holder of reason and law, but the Master of Noise. The exercise of power is based on media simulation and nervous stimulation.

What should we do in such a situation? Should we reclaim the re-establishment of the authority of Logos, which was once based on the slow circulation of semiotic stimulations? Should we reclaim respect for the rational force of the law? Should we reclaim the authenticity of the public discourse?

I don't think so.

I don't deny that the amount of purely false information is growing, or that it is detrimental to democracy and useful for the bad guys. But false information is not a novelty in public discourse. What is new is the speed, the intensity and therefore the enormous amount of information (fake or otherwise) that the average mind is exposed to.

The problem is the decomposition of the social brain, the acceleration of the info-sphere, and the extreme intensification of the rhythm of semiotic stimulation.

Critical skills are not a natural given, but the result of

AUTHENTICITY?

mental evolution in history. The cognitive faculty that we name *critique* develops only under special conditions. Critique is the individual ability to distinguish between false and true enunciations, and also to distinguish between right and wrong.

The mind needs time to process information in a critical way. Critical thinking implies a rhythmic relation between info-stimulus and elaboration.

Beyond a certain intensity, info-stimulation is received and interpreted, not as a complex of enunciations, but as a flow of nervous stimulations: an emotional assault on the brain.

The critical faculty that was crucial to the formation of public opinion in the bourgeois period was the effect of a special relation between the individual mind and the infosphere, particularly those domains in which books and newspapers circulated and public discussions took place.

The mind was engaged to work its way through a slow flux of words sequentially disposed on the page, so the public discourse was a space of conscious evaluations and critical discriminations, and political choice was based on critical assessment and ideological discernment.

The acceleration of the info-flow led to the saturation of the social mind, so that the ability to discriminate between true and false became impossible, the deluge of info-stimulation blurred people's vision, and people tended to wrap themselves in networks of self-confirmation.

The Internet has evolved into a space where the same messages reverberate in countless echo chambers: competition, identity, aggressiveness.

As far as I can tell, the main problem with the contemporary mediascape is not the spread of fake news, but the decomposition of the critical mind whose effects are the gullibility of the masses and the self-affirming aggressiveness of citizens.

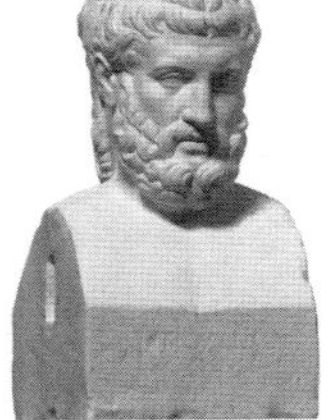

Advertising is the defining language of the present mediascape, and the effectiveness or otherwise of advertising messages is based, not on truth or critical reception, but on the intensity of nervous stimulation.

The cultural regression of our time is not rooted in the growth of false information. It is, rather, an effect of the inability of the social mind to elaborate critical distinctions, the inability of people to prioritize their own social experience, and to create a common pathway of autonomous subjectivation. This is why people vote for media manipulators who exploit their gullibility.

Simulation and Identity

What do we mean when we speak of 'reality'? What is a 'fact'?

A fact is what has been made in the sphere of human conventions (*facere* is the Latin word that means 'to make'). Facts are the products of factual semiosis by people. And reality is the psychodynamic point of intersection of countless projections of simulation flows proceeding from human organisms and from semiotic machines.

Social reality does not pre-exist to the act of semiosis and of communication.

Reality is the construct emanating from multiple subjectivities: power, social rebellion, political imagination, and art experiments. Power, in fact, is the fixation of a set of expressive simulations in form of institutions, laws, and established relations. The fixation of the enunciative flow of simulation into established forms of perception and projection may be labelled Gestalt, in the precise sense that Gestalt psychologists gave to the term: a form that generates forms, while fixating and reproducing the prevailing *rapport de force* in the sphere of perception. Paraphrasing Wittgenstein, one may say that the limits of the established language are limits of the established world, not the limits of the possible world. Possible worlds diverge from the established Gestalt, and emanate from diverging subjectivities.

'There is nothing more fictitious than reality' says Umberto Eco in an interview with Alex Coles entitled *Here*

4

Alex Coles, ed., *EP Vol. 2: Design Fiction* (Berlin, 2016).

I am, not a fiction in the book *Design Fiction.*[4] The whole debate about post-truth is based on a philosophical misunderstanding that primarily concerns the very notion of truth and authenticity in the present techno-media landscape.

The technological transition that is underway is not provoking a collapse of truth and authenticity, but is bringing about a radical reframing of the relation between media and self-perception. Therefore, I want to sketch the lines of this mutation at three levels—between us and:

* the territory
* others' bodies
* our selves

At the first level, let's consider the transformations that GPS technology can induce in our sense of direction—which is based on our ability to remember sights, nuances, smells, and colours, as well as on the creation of interior maps. We may legitimately expect that the use of GPS will affect the very ability to remember our surroundings. Map and territory tend to overlap in our mental space: we are no longer traversing territories. We are, rather, following the instructions on a map.

Maps are taking the place of territory, but they are in fact the fixation of our previous experience of the territory.

The second level concerns our relation to others' bodies. We send and receive information about those others, but we are not dealing with their presence. The others are implicated as a linguistic fiction, not as bodies. This mutation is rooted in our growing inability to show solidarity with the social body.

The third level concerns our relation to ourselves.

A reframing of self-perception comes together with the datafication of the identity. Our identity is increasingly becoming a construct that comprises the data we exude. These data objectify our identity,

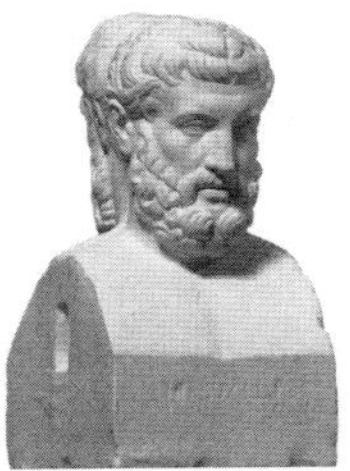

　　　　TRAP OF IDENTITY AND DELUSION OF TRUTH

fix the ever-shuffling process of individuation, and immobilize the continual process of our re-definition.

Identification always implies the creation of an imaginary mirror, but in the sphere of datafication, the screen takes the place of the mirror. The screen conveys flows of information about us and is transformed as a reification of our identity into a sort of eternalization of the perception of the mirror. All attempts to stabilize and secure identity imply some degree of self-violence that finally turns into aggression.

I think there is no identity: there are processes of identification.

Identification is a way to stabilize reflexive consciousness. It acts, in the end, as a projection of reflexive consciousness. This stabilization is always provisional and swiftly fades away, but the will to identity leads to aggressive forms of differentiation from the environment. Identification may be viewed as an attempt to stabilize the self in its relation with outside reality. Fascism is the obsessive and aggressive enforcement of that provisional stabilization.

'Observing his subatomic self no chronology was stable', writes Jonathan Franzen in *Purity,* a novel that may be read as an attempt to outline simultaneously a genealogy of contemporary depression and of contemporary Fascism.

Identity as a Political Trap

The novels of Franzen are, in my opinion, not only a wonderful literary achievement but also a political diagnosis of the effects of the global deterritorialization that provokes a loss of identity and that then leads to aggressive forms of reterritorialization: racism, nationalism, religious fanaticism and so on may be read as dangerous attempts to rebuild a sense of belonging based on a false concept of identity.

Identity is a conceptual trap: it does not exists, but it produces mirror effects—the result of looking back longingly at some imagined origin. The fixation of the identified self often happens through the identification of the other and the differentiation from the identified other.

The origin of contemporary aggressiveness and fascism rest on this ontologization of the self (which also takes on 'ethnic' or religious or national features). The conviction that identity is a natural (and thus 'authentic') starting point for the existence of the individual is the conceptual nucleus of the aggressive identity politics that is currently jeopardising democracy and humanism.

The contemporary crisis of the European Union is the consequence of the impoverishment of social life produced by financial predation, but at the same time it has also resulted from the resurfacing of identitarian nationalism. Because European culture has been unable to invent a form of the Union that is emancipated from the need for identification, we are now dissipating the legacy of the Enlightenment and of socialism, and are once again entering the tunnel of war.

In his 1933 book, *Discours à la nation européenne*, Julien Benda wrote that, if one wants to be European one cannot *start* from being European, because in fact there is no such thing as being European. Being European is an oxymoron, because Europe is not an ontological given, or a unified identity. Rather, it is a space of permanent becoming, of conflict and miscegenation and contamination.

You may say that French and German identity exist. But you cannot say that there is something like a 'European' identity. Benda thus concludes that, if one wants to create a European entity one must know that it can only be the product of your spirit, of your mind, of your will.

Europe is a project that can be based only on the concatenation of difference and the cooperation of minds. If we want to understand the richness of the European project, we must realize that it can be based only on forgetting identity.

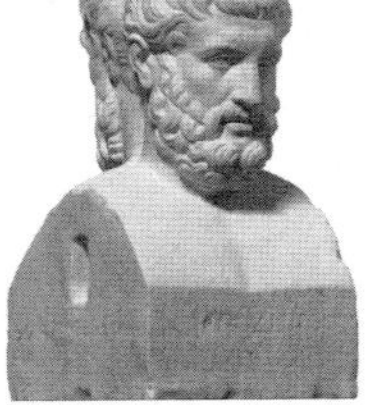

   TRAP OF IDENTITY AND DELUSION OF TRUTH

CONTRIBUTORS

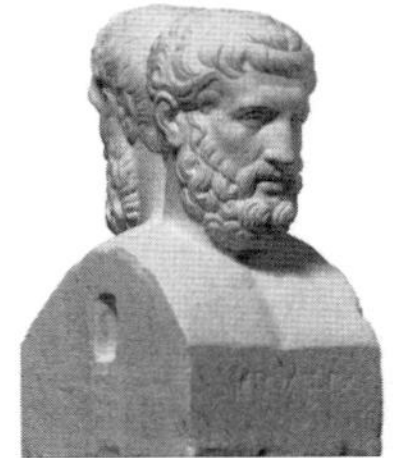

ERIKA BALSOM is Senior Lecturer in Film Studies and Liberal Arts at King's College, London. She holds an MA in Cultural Studies from Goldsmiths College, London, and a PhD in Modern Culture and Media from Brown University in Providence, RI (US). Her research interests include experimental documentaries, media archaeology, and exhibition history. Her writing has appeared in journals such as *Cinema Journal*, *Screen*, and *Afterall*, and her study of the moving image in art since 1990, *Exhibiting Cinema in Contemporary Art*, was published by Amsterdam University Press in 2013.

FRANCO 'BIFO' BERARDI is a renowned theorist of contemporary media, culture and society. In 1976 he founded Radio Alice. He is one of the most prominent members of Autonomia. Recent books include *The Soul at Work: From Alienation to Autonomy*; *The Uprising: On Poetry and Finance*; and *And Phenomenology of the End*. In his work, Berardi explores the role that media and technology play in post-industrial capitalism, and examines issues such as digital connectivity, alienation, over-stimulation and automation. Central to his work is an ongoing study of cultural representation and our ideas of the future.

BARBARA CUETO & BAS HENDRIKX met when they were both taking part in the curatorial programme of De Appel arts centre in Amsterdam. In collaboration with Lian Ladia, they curated 'Your Time Is Not My Time' (2015) at De Appel. They were curators of the Impakt Festival 2016, and the exhibition 'Running Time' (2016) at Marres, a house for contemporary culture in Maastricht (NL).

Cueto co-founded the Vesselroom Project in Berlin in 2014, and has served as a curatorial fellow at Bétonsalon in Paris. Upcoming projects include 'Atlas for Uncertain Futures' at the National Museum of Modern and Contemporary Art in Seoul, and Tokyo Wondersite, and 'I Would Prefer Not To' at La Casa Encendida in Madrid.

Hendrikx is the former associate curator at P/////AKT in Amsterdam, and was curator at Hotel Maria Kapel in Hoorn (NL). Recent projects include 'The Queer Series' and the exhibition 'Hybrid Modus' for Skulptur Bredelar in Bredelar (GE).

MATHEW DRYHURST & HOLLY HERNDON work together regularly. In 2015, they staged the exhibition 'Everywhere and Nowhere' at Kunstverein Hamburg. Their music is released by the Berlin-based record label PAN.

Dryhurst, an artist, developed the online distribution tool Saga, which allows artists to own the spaces where their work is hosted online. Recently he premiered MUSTER, an audio play derived entirely from data-mining the listenership of Deutschland Radio Kultur.

Herndon was born and raised in Johnson City, TN (US), and was part of the Berlin minimal techno scene before moving to San Francisco to do a PhD at Stanford's Center for Computer Research in Music and Acoustics. She recently released her second album, *Platform*, on RVNG Intl./4AD. She performs around the world, and has recently installed work at the Palais de Tokyo in Paris and the Guggenheim in New York City.

JAZMINA FIGUEROA is an independent researcher based in Berlin. Her areas of focus range from activism to artists' rights and the preservation of new media. Previously she worked in digital-rights advocacy and with blockchain technologies that help protect intellectual property and copyright for artists. From 2013 to 2016 she curated exhibitions, and held screenings and workshops, in Berlin and London. She has also screened her own work at the South London Gallery, London

ROB HORNING is an editor at *Real Life Magazine* and a contributing editor of *The New Inquiry*. His writing has also appeared

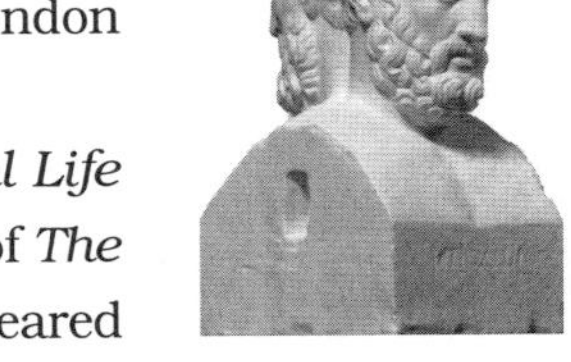

CONTRIBUTORS

in *Time Out New York* and *Skyscraper*. In his *PopMatters* column, 'Marginal Utility', he bridges the abstract and concrete aspects of consumerism. He holds a BA and an MA in English Literature. In his 2009 article 'The Death of the Hipster', he argues that the hipster might be the 'embodiment of postmodernism as a spent force, revealing what happens when pastiche and irony exhaust themselves as aesthetics'.

DAVID JOSELIT is a historian, critic, educator and former curator. His art-historical work has approached the history and theory of image circulation in the twentieth and twenty-first centuries from a variety of perspectives, from Marcel Duchamp's strategy of the readymade to the mid-twentieth-century ecology of television, video art and media activism and the current conditions of contemporary art under the dual pressures of globalization and digitization. Joselit is a Distinguished Professor at The Graduate Center at the City University of New York. His published work includes the book *After Art* and the article 'Painting Beside Itself'. He is an editor at the journal *October* and a regular contributor to *Artforum*.

OLIVER LARIC's work examines historical and contemporary ideas related to image hierarchies. He proposes that current methods of creative production challenge the hierarchy of an authentic or auratic 'original' image. The interplay between, and issues surrounding, authenticity and distribution are at the core of Laric's work. He seamlessly displays the paradoxical positions artists are faced with, and comes up with challenging new proposals on how to address these.

TIMOTHEUS VERMEULEN is an Associate Professor of Media, Culture and Society at the University of Oslo, Norway. With Robin van den Akker, he is the author of the essay *Notes on Metamodernism,* and the founder of the arts and culture platform of the same name. He has published in *The Journal of Aesthetics and Culture, Screen, Monu, The American Book*

Review, *e-flux Journal*, *Frieze*, and *Texte zur Kunst*, among others. He is the author of the monograph *Scenes from the Suburbs*, published by Edinburgh University Press in 2014, and joint editor, with Martin Dines, of *New Suburban Stories*, published by Bloomsbury in 2013. He is the joint editor, with Robin van den Akker and Alison Gibbons, of *Metamodernism: Historicity, Affect and Depth after Postmodernism*, forthcoming from Rowman & Littlefield.

BENY WAGNER is an artist working in the moving image, text, installation and lectures. Combining research and speculation to form non-linear narratives, he investigates the many modes of mediation between the self and its surroundings, whether in technology, agriculture, ecology, or material and virtual space. A recurring preoccupation in his work is the politics and ethics of vision and representation: he looks specifically at how language and technology give shape to the boundaries of social consciousness. His recent show at Van Eyck in Maastricht (NL), examined the pseudo-intimate relations between an Airbnb tenant and his host: his work pointed up a casual yet awkward familiarity between two practical strangers as they each played their roles, which involved both intimacy and sincerity. It also the highlighted visual languages that accompanied these relations. Wagner graduated from Bard College in New York City, and was a participant at the Van Eyck Multiform Institute for Fine Art, Design and Reflection.

MCKENZIE WARK is Professor and Chair of Culture and Media at The New School in New York City. He is known for his writings on critical and media theory and on the Situationist International. Publications include *The Spectacle of Disintegration, The Beach Beneath the Street: The Everyday Like and Glorious Times of the Situationist International*, and *A Hacker Manifesto*.

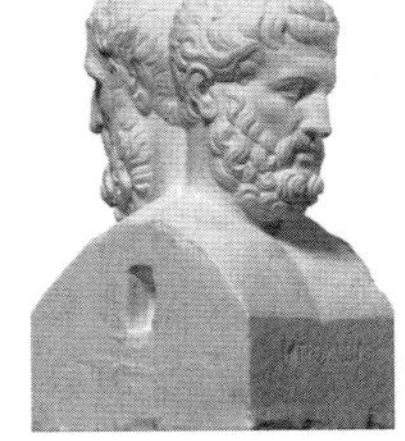

INDEX OF NAMES

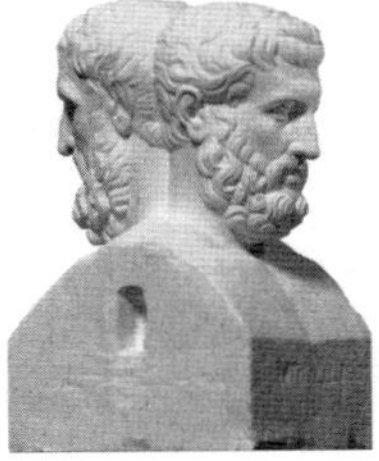

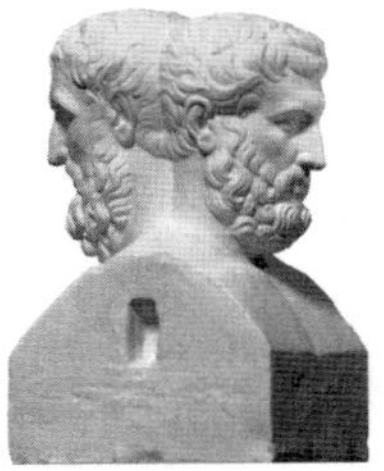

INDEX OF NAMES

IMPAKT

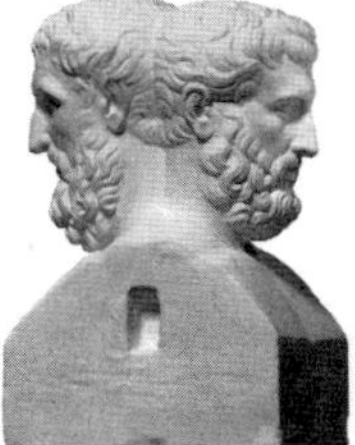

Authenticity? Observations and Artistic Strategies in the Post-Digital Age was produced by Impakt and Valiz as a spin-off from the Impakt Festival 2016, entitled 'Authenticity?' The editors of the present volume, Barbara Cueto and Bas Hendrikx, were the curators of the 2016 festival, and this volume includes contributions by many of the artists and speakers featured in the festival programme.

IMPAKT CRITICAL AND CREATIVE VIEWS ON MEDIA CULTURE

Impakt presents critical and creative views on contemporary media culture and on innovative audio-visual arts in an inter-disciplinary context. Impakt examines issues around society, digital culture, and media from various angles and within a range of disciplines in the arts, academia, and technology.

Our main project is the annual Impakt Festival, a five-day multimedia event that includes exhibitions, film screenings, lectures, panels, performances, presentations, and artists' talks at locations in Utrecht, the Netherlands.

We organize activities throughout the year, including Impakt Works, a residency programme, and Impakt Events, a regular series of presentations and screenings centring on a given theme, movement, or artist. The Impakt Channel is a platform where art projects made for the internet are presented, along with curated programmes featuring film and video art. Last but not least, the Impakt Archive works on digitising Impakt's screening history back to 1988, when the first Impakt Festival was organized.

The 2017 festival takes place at the end of October and its theme is Haunted Machines, Wicked Problems. Curators Natalie Kane and Tobias Revell will map the relationships among technology, mythology, and magic.

www.impakt.nl
info@impakt.nl

PO Box 735
3500 AS Utrecht
The Netherlands

COLOPHON

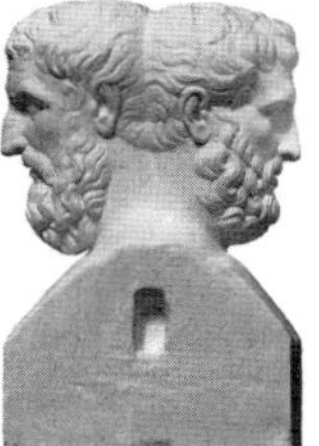

Editors: Barbara Cueto, Bas Hendrikx
Contributors: Erika Balsom, Franco 'Bifo'
Berardi, Barbara Cueto & Bas Hendrikx,
Jazmina Figueroa, Holly Herndon &
Mat Dryhurst, Rob Horning, David Joselit,
Oliver Laric, Timotheus Vermeulen,
Beny Wagner, McKenzie Wark

Copy-editing: Ciarán Ó Faoláin
Proofreading: Els Brinkman
Index: Elke Stevens
Graphic design: Template,
www.template01.info
Typefaces: Tex Gyre Bonum, Tex Gyre Chorus
Paper inside: Munken Print White, 100 gr
Paper cover: Bioset 240 gr
Printing: Bariet-Ten Brink, Meppel
Publisher: Astrid Vorstermans / Valiz,
Amsterdam, 2017, www.valiz.nl with
Impakt Foundation, Utrecht, www.impakt.nl

This publication is connected to the *Impakt
Festival 2016: Authenticity?* that was supported
by the City of Utrecht, Creative Industries Fund
NL, Mondriaan Fund, Fonds 21, K.F. Hein Fonds,
VSBfonds and the Fentener van Vlissingen Fonds.

Thanks to: Impakt staff and volunteers,
Kasper Bosmans, Harm van den Dorpel,
Gerard Loozekoot, Ilga Minjon, Gieneke Pieterse,
Britte Sloothaak, Pieter Verbeke.

The editors and the publisher have made every
effort to secure permission to reproduce the
listed material, texts and illustrations. We apolo-
gize for any inadvert errors or omissions. Parties
who nevertheless believe they can claim specific
legal rights are invited to contact the publisher.
info@valiz.nl

INTERNATIONAL DISTRIBUTION
BE/NL/LU: Coen Sligting,
www.coensligtingbookimport.nl;
Centraal Boekhuis,
www.centraal.boekhuis.nl
GB/IE: Anagram Books,
www.anagrambooks.com
Europe (excl GB/IE)/Asia:
Idea Books, www.ideabooks.nl
Australia: Perimeter,
www.perimeterdistribution.com
USA, Canada, Latin-America: D.A.P.,
www.artbook.com
Individual orders:
www.valiz.nl; info@valiz.nl

ISBN 978-94-92095-23-7
Printed and bound in the EU